GRUESOME DEATHS
AND CELIBATE LIVES

Christian Martyrs and Ascetics

GREECE & ROME LIVE
Also available or forthcoming in this series:

Ancient Greece in Film and Popular Culture, Gideon Nisbet
Augustine: The Confessions, Gillian Clark
Augustus: Caesar's Web: Power & Propaganda in Augustan Rome, Matthew
    H.C. Clark
Catullus, John Godwin
Epic Poetry after Virgil, Robert Cowan
Greek Tyranny, Sian Lewis
Hadrian's Wall and Its People, Geraint Osborn
Inside the Greek House, Janett Morgan
Julius Caesar, Robert Garland
The Law in Ancient Greece, Christopher Carey
The Law of Rome, Jane Gardner
Pausanias: the Ancient Guide to Greece, John Taylor
The Politics of Greek Tragedy, David M. Carter
Sophocles, James Morwood
Story and Spectacle: Rome at the Cinema, Elena Theodorakopoulos
The Trojan War, Emma Stafford

GRUESOME DEATHS AND CELIBATE LIVES

Christian Martyrs and Ascetics

Aideen M. Hartney

BRISTOL
PHOENIX
PRESS

Cover illustration: J.W. Waterhouse, Saint Eulalia;
© Tate, London 2004

First published in 2005 by
Bristol Phoenix Press
an imprint of The Exeter Press
Reed Hall, Streatham Drive,
Exeter, Devon, EX4 4QR
UK

www.exeterpress.co.uk

© Aideen M. Hartney 2005

British Library Cataloguing in Publication Data
A catalogue record for this book is available
from the British Library.

ISBN 1-904675-13-1 (Paperback)
ISBN 1-904675-42-5 (Hardback)

Printed and bound by CPI Group (UK) Ltd, Croydon, CR0 4YY

For Simon
with love and thanks

Contents

Preface ix

Roman Emperors and their Years of Reign xi

Map of the World of Late Antiquity xvi

1 Pagans and Christians: Introduction 1

2 Periods of Persecution 15

3 The Language of Suffering and Death 33

4 The Survival of the Church 51

5 The Rise of the Holy Person in Late Antiquity 59

6 Ascetics and Church Ministry 79

7 The Female Road to Redemption 91

8 'Illegal' Forms of Asceticism 111

Conclusions 121

Notes 129

Further Reading 135

Index 139

Preface

Christianity has become one of the dominant world religions but its origins belie its present position of power. In its very earliest years Christians were outlawed and persecuted by the secular authorities of the day. Even when it grew to be accepted as a legitimate religious system, the Church, divided by factions and opposing beliefs, failed to achieve an over-night conversion of the Roman world. Within this turbulent period, however, various Christians emerged from among the ranks of the faithful to seize the imagination and hold the attention of the rest of their communities. They were those who were willing to die for their faith as martyrs or those who tried to subsume their physical desires and needs to spiritual ends as ascetics or holy people.

This book aims to provide a brief introduction to these issues and to the thinking behind martyrdom and asceticism, key elements that defined early Christianity. The extent of the volume precludes detailed discussion or inclusion of many portraits of the individuals involved. Yet it is to be hoped that some of these brief sketches will whet the appetite of readers, who may be encouraged to look further into a fascinating period of history. It is one that sheds light, not only on the way in which the Christian Church subsequently developed, but also on the changes within the society of antiquity that resulted from the decline of the Roman empire. The personalities involved are intriguing, largely because their behaviour was so extreme; but such extremes have been incorporated into Christian doctrine – and have influenced standards of sanctity ever since.

The rise of Christianity within the Roman empire is the primary focus of this work, which means that I have treated the 'fall' of this empire as a natural boundary for my discussion. While I am wary of speaking in terms of an abrupt collapse of the Roman empire that happened all at once, it is nevertheless true that by the end of the fifth century AD the western half of the empire began to go a very separate way from its eastern counterpart. The east began to merge into the Byzantine empire and a very different period of history. The Christian Church in the east also underwent changes and adjustments and ultimately developed into what would be more recognisable as a version of eastern Orthodox Christianity than the western form with which many of us may be more familiar. Given these sharp distinctions, I have chosen not to take my study into these areas and hope that readers will not be overly frustrated by this. Byzantine history and eastern Orthodoxy are detailed areas of study in their own right – ones I am not equipped to do justice to in this volume. My own Catholic influences must also be acknowledged at this point, as they are an inevitable part of the way in which I view the Church and its early history and should therefore be signposted at the outset (for the benefit of those who do not bear similar baggage).

I would like to take this opportunity to thank all those who have advised me throughout my studies of late antiquity: Gillian Clark, Theresa Urbainczyk and John Davies. I would also like to thank John Betts for offering me the opportunity to make such a compelling period of history accessible to a wider audience. Family and friends have also been constantly supportive; but most particular thanks must go to Simon Spence for his steadfast friendship and invaluable help.

Roman Emperors
and their Years of Reign

- Augustus (27 BC - AD 14)
- Tiberius (AD 14-37)
- Gaius Caligula (AD 37-41)
- Claudius (AD 41-54)
- Nero (AD 54-68)
- Galba (AD 68-9)
- Otho (AD 69)
- Vitellius (AD 69)
- Vespasian (AD 69-79)
- Titus Flavius (AD 79-81)
- Domitian (AD 81-96)
- Nerva (AD 96-8)
- Trajan (AD 98-117)
- Hadrian (AD 117-38)
- Antoninus Pius (AD 138-61)
- Marcus Aurelius (AD 161-80) (co-emperor Lucius Verus AD 161-9)
- Commodus (AD 180-193)
- Pertinax (AD 193)
- Septimius Severus (AD 193-211)
- Caracalla (AD 211-17)
- Macrinus (AD 217-18)
- Elagabalus (AD 218-22)
- Alexander Severus (AD 222-35)

Rulers during the 'Third Century Crisis'

- Maximinus Thrax (AD 235-8)
- Gordian I and Gordian II (AD 238)
- Pupienus and Balbinus (AD 238)
- Gordian III (AD 238-44) (throne claimed by Sabinianus AD 240)
- Philip the Arab (AD 244-9) (throne claimed by Pacantius AD 248, Iotapianus 248, and Silbannacus)
- Decius (AD 249-51) (throne claimed by Priscus AD 249-52; and Licinianus 250)
- Herennius Etruscus (AD 251)
- Hostilian (AD 251)
- Trebonianus Gallus (AD 251-3)
- Aemilianus (AD 253)
- Valerian I (AD 253-260)
- Gallienus (AD 260-8) (throne claimed by Ingenuus 260; Regalianus 260; Macrianus Major, Macrianus Minor and Quietus 260 – 1; Mussius Aemilianus 261-2; and Aureolus 268)
- Claudius II Gothicus (AD 268-270)
- Quintillus (AD 270)
- Aurelian (AD 270-5) (throne claimed by Domitianus 270-1; and Septimius 271)
- Tacitus (AD 275-6)
- Florianus (AD 276)
- Probus (AD 276-282) (throne claimed by Saturninus 280; Proculus 280; and Bonosus 280)
- Carus (AD 282-3)
- Carinus (AD 283-5) (co-emperor Numerian)

The Tetrarchy

- Diocletian (AD 284-305) (co-emperor Maximian AD 286-305)
- Constantius Chlorus (AD 305-6) (co-emperor Galerius AD 305-11)
- Constantine I, the Great (AD 306-37) (co-emperors Galerius, Licinius AD 308-24 and Maximin AD 308-13)
- Constantius II (AD 337-61) (together with Constantine II 337-40 and Constans 337-50)
- Julian (AD 361-3) (also known as 'the Apostate')
- Jovian (AD 363-4)
- Valentinian I (AD 364-75) (co-emperor Valens 364-78; throne claimed by Procopius 364-5)
- Gratianus (AD 375-83) (co-emperor Valentinian II 375-92)
- Theodosius I (AD 379-95)

The Western Empire

- Honorius (AD 395-423) (co-emperor Constantius III 421)
- Valentinian III (AD 423-55)
- Petronius Maximus (AD 455)
- Avitus (AD 456-7)
- Majorian (AD 457-61)
- Libius Severus (AD 461-65)
- Anthemius (AD 467-72)
- Olybrius (AD 472)
- Glycerius (AD 473-4)
- Julius Nepos-(AD 474-75/80)
- Romulus Augustus (a.k.a. Romulus Augustulus), 'last' western emperor (AD 475-6)

The Eastern Empire

- Arcadius (AD 395-408)
- Theodosius II (AD 408-50)
- Marcian (AD 450-7)
- Leo I (AD 457-74)
- Leo II (AD 474)
- Zeno (AD 474-91)
- Basiliscus (AD 475-76)
- Anastasius I, (AD 491-518)
- Justin I the Great, (AD 518-27)
- Justinian I the Great, (AD 527-65)
- Justin II, (AD 565-78)
- Tiberius II Constantine, (AD 578-82)
- Maurice I Tiberius, (AD 582-602)
- Phocas the Tyrant, (AD 602-10)
- Heraclius, (AD 610-41)
- Constantine III Heraclius, (AD 641)
- Heraclonas Constantine, (AD 641)
- Constans II Heraclius Pogonatus (the Bearded), (AD 641-68)
- Constantine IV, (AD 668-85)
- Justinian II Rhinotmetus (the Slit-nosed), (AD 685-95)
- Leontius II, (AD 695-98)
- Tiberius III Apsimar (AD 698-705)
- Justinian II, Rhinotmetus (restored, second rule AD 705-11)
- Philippicus Bardanes, (AD 711-13)
- Anastasius II, (AD 713-15)
- Theodosius III, (AD 715-17)

BRITAIN
York

GAUL
ALAMANNI
Tours
Lyons
Vienne
Milan
DALMATIA
Milvian Bridge
Ostia Rome
Merida
Seville
Carthage
Thagaste
AFRICA
Lepcis Magna

THE WORLD OF LATE ANTIQUITY

BLACK SEA

Adrianople
hessalonica
Constantinople
Chalcedon
BITHYNIA-PONTUS
CAPPADOCIA
Nyssa• •Caesarea
PHRYGIA
Nazianzus
Tarsus•
•Antioch
SYRIA •Palmyra
MEDITERRANEAN SEA
•Tyre
• Jerusalem
•Bethlehem
Alexandria
Gaza
EGYPT
•Medina
Thebes•
RED SEA
•Mecca
CASPIAN SEA

Chapter 1

Pagans and Christians: Introduction

Felicity obtained great grace from the Lord. She was eight
months pregnant at the time of her arrest. When the day of
the games approached, she was saddened by the thought that
they would put off her martyrdom because of her state, since
the law prohibited the execution of pregnant women. She
was also afraid that she would later have to shed her pure and
spotless blood among a horde of criminals. Her companions
in martyrdom were saddened by the thought of leaving such
a good companion alone, a friend who was journeying with
them towards the same hope.

(*The Martyrdom of Saints Perpetua and Felicity,* ch. 15)

There in the desert Antony was a daily martyr to his conscience, and was constantly engaged in battles for the sake
of his faith. And his discipline was very severe, for he was
constantly fasting, and he had a garment which had hair on
the inside, while the outside was skin, which he wore until
his death. And he neither bathed his body with water to free
himself from filth, nor did he ever wash his feet, nor even
endure so much as to put them into water, unless it became
absolutely necessary. Nor did any one ever see him without
his clothes, nor see his body naked, except after his death,
when he was buried. (*Life of St. Antony*, ch. 47)

These two accounts of the lives of saints were penned roughly a
hundred and fifty years apart. They shed light on two different,
but related, styles of Christian living in the later Roman empire.
In the first instance, Felicity (*d.* AD 203) was one of many early
Christians who were martyred because of their allegiance to the
faith in defiance of Roman authorities. Antony (AD 251-356), on

1

the other hand, is widely regarded as the father of the Christian 'holy men' or ascetics, who may in turn be seen as the forerunners of a more recognisable monasticism such as still exists today. One was a female slave to a wealthy family in the city of Carthage, the other a poorly educated farmer's son from Egypt. Even coming from such different backgrounds and living their lives in seemingly disparate ways, both Felicity and Antony served as shining examples and role models for the rest of their Christian brethren, as well as providing fascinating and entertaining tales of endurance for pagan and Christian audiences alike.

Felicity and Antony – and many others like them – stimulated contemporary popular imagination because of the courage of their convictions and the extreme nature of their resulting actions. They may seem odd to us today because of those extremes, willing either to die or to starve themselves in their quest for spiritual salvation. Yet such was the power of their behaviour that they became incorporated into the Christian Church as recognisably holy – as saints – and, as such, are still venerated today.

The purpose of this book is to explain why such characters ended up acting as they did and how they influenced the society around them. How could a young female slave, newly a mother, cheerfully embrace a gruesome death in the Roman arena? How was a farmer's son able to turn his back on his inheritance and his surviving family and willingly adopt a life of isolation and deprivation in the desert? What was it about the society of the day that prompted – even facilitated – such extreme behaviour? What was it about the Christian religion that particularly lent itself to such dramatic demonstrations of faith? And what were the changing circumstances that gave martyrdom a limited period of relevance and led to the rise of asceticism in its place?

One might argue that the very origins of Christianity laid down a blueprint for self-sacrifice and martyrdom. Jesus Christ himself had been crucified by the Roman authorities in Palestine at the instigation of local Jewish leaders, who had felt threatened by the philosophies behind his preaching and by the significant public following he enjoyed. Jesus' immediate followers – his apostles – regarded his death as a voluntary act of self-sacrifice for the sake of the greater good. This interpretation quickly became a theological cornerstone of the fledgling religion, followed, as it was, by the story of Jesus' resurrection and ascension into heaven. His willingness to die for others was presented to new members of the Church as the adoption of an intercessionary role between themselves, as ordinary mortals, and the divine authority of God the Father. Such an act of martyrdom conferred greater power on the martyr and, at the same time, benefited those who remained behind. This was one of the reasons why Christian martyrdom achieved such a level of notice and became so crucial an element in the history of the early Church. It was not a uniquely Christian concept; for Jewish religion had produced its own martyrs, who were presented as shining lights of example to the rest of their society. Of these figures the best known were the Maccabees (*ca* 63–70 BC), who were tortured and executed for refusing to deny the precepts of their religion by eating pork (4 Macabees 5-17). The command to break this key tenet of Jewish law had come from a tyrant, Antiochus; those who refused to do his bidding claimed to be following divine law handed down from God. The story of their tortures pre-figures many of the motifs we find in traditional Christian martyr texts. Similar, too, was the firm belief that their deaths would be vindicated by God and that he was willing to bring them to salvation as reward for their faith and obedience. The addresses made to the tyrant by each martyr, their steadfast adherence to the letter of their divine law and the assurance they felt that they were doing God's will – are all echoed in later Christian hagiographies. Even the sense in which the seven brothers of the account and their mother offer support to each other, enabling them to face death unwavering, is something we will also find in Christian examples.

So martyrdom for reasons of belief was not a Christian invention. However, Christian martyrs seized the popular imagination in a way in which their predecessors had not. In the first place there were many more of them and they were not confined to a single region or province of the empire but found throughout Rome's territory. Christianity also seized on the notion that martyrs, on account of their glorious and holy deaths, became able to intercede in heaven for those left behind on earth, assisting others on their own road to salvation. Thus an 'eternal' dimension was brought to bear on the concept of martyrdom where previous examples had concentrated only on the manner of the death and the fact that it was willingly embraced. The Christian martyrs, therefore, had a life and an importance far beyond their actual deaths and it is this that keeps them so firmly in the consciousness of the Church.

In the very earliest years of the Church this pattern, begun in the time of the Maccabees and realised in the person of Jesus, continued as Christ's followers were sometimes persecuted and executed for their professed beliefs. It began to be presented as a great honour to be so selected for mistreatment; it was an emulation of the courage and selflessness of the religion's founder. So a tradition of admiration and celebration of such deaths came into being and proved a defining aspect of almost the first 300 years of Christianity. Of course for martyrs to exist there is need for a persecutor, and in the case of Christianity this took the form of the might of the Roman empire. Traditional Roman religion was very different both in ethos and in practice from Christianity but it was considered crucial to the survival and continued prosperity of the empire itself. Christianity therefore posed a grave threat to everything the ordinary Roman believed in and held dear.

Traditional Roman religion

At the time when Christianity as a way of life was beginning to take hold, the Roman empire extended throughout the Mediterranean world and into Asia. A variety of different races and beliefs were incorporated within this over-arching society and one of Rome's greatest achievements was that it had managed to reconcile so many disparate elements relatively smoothly for such a length of time. The key to her success in this regard lay in the way in which she treated religious matters. Rome professed belief in a polytheistic religious system with a pantheon of gods who could deal with any and every eventuality. They had gods for the city walls and for the domestic hearth, gods who guarded against the attack of enemies and gods who guarded against specific diseases that could blight crops. There was a god of doorways, a god of the bedroom, and separate gods for fertility in nature and for fertility among humans. There is an old joke that shows the extent to which Roman life was permeated by their allegiance to these gods: 'if the Romans had invented the bicycle, they would have had a goddess Punctura!' It may not be a very good joke; but it indicates the importance attached by Romans to the observance of religious rituals and to the designation of a deity for every public and private space involved in daily life. Public display of piety was seen as essential for the continued prosperity of society. Romans offered prayers and sacrifices to their gods for the safety of the family and the household; also for the fertility of the soil, the success of the harvest, victory in battle, prosperity in peace-time and, overall, the continued security of the society which they had built. Non-Christian Romans are often described as 'pagans' – a word which has come to be interpreted as lacking religious belief. In fact paganism more accurately describes this 'traditional' system of prayers and offerings made to a whole population of deities in return for continued well-being.

These prayers and offerings were generally public in nature and the Romans had a very full religious calendar. Public festivals and feast days were built around many of the religious observances, providing an opportunity for members of the society to observe their own success and to pray for its perpetuation. These religious rites were more about demonstrating loyalty to the concept of the Roman empire than they were about theology or an ethical life-style. Guidance on morality and the appropriate way to behave was derived instead from philosophers and their various schools of thought. So, for example, the Stoics taught that one must bear the vicissitudes of life with equanimity, that this was the path to virtuous living. The Epicureans, on the other hand, believed that life was transitory, that the manner in which it was lived counted for little in the hereafter; and from this attitude derived their 'eat, drink and be merry, for tomorrow we die', approach.

One's adherence to a particular set of philosophical beliefs was of little interest to the outside world, however, – and certainly not to the Roman authorities. Provided citizens of Rome were obedient in civil matters, maintaining the religious observances that were seen as vital for the preservation of the empire as a structure, private beliefs remained private. It is entirely possible, therefore, that many Roman citizens went about their daily business, including the many small religious rites and rituals that this involved, with very little thought for a larger scheme of theology or for a particular morality.

This was how Rome managed to retain its position of power over so many different societies and ethnicities. Since one's theological or moral beliefs were largely a matter for oneself, the Roman authorities did not have to worry about how to incorporate any radically different religious beliefs into their system. Instead they imposed their publicly observed system on newly conquered or absorbed peoples from outside, leaving them free to practice a tiered approach to religion. Once people agreed to adopt the Roman religious observances, they were free to retain or discard their original beliefs and practices as they saw fit.

Thus Roman religion became ever more a demonstration of allegiance to the empire – and even to the emperor. Following the deification of the first emperor Augustus, it became regular practice to declare the emperor a god – either after or before his death. Once again, a willingness to profess this belief in public came to be equated with a willingness to belong to Roman society and to uphold its values. It became even more important for newly absorbed societies to follow suit; for this was their acknowledgement of the emperor as their new source of authority. So sacrifices were offered to the Roman emperor at regular intervals; his continued well-being was regarded as indivisible from that of the state as a whole.

Again citizen and non-citizen alike were free to observe their own religious beliefs in tandem with their public demonstrations of loyalty. So there was no head-on clash of belief-systems of the sort that might have been divisive or disruptive for the empire. This carefully maintained balance broke down with the annexation of Judea and the Jewish people.

The threat of monotheism

Judaism, the direct precursor to Christianity, was somewhat unusual in the Roman world by reason of its rigid monotheism. Jews believed in only one god – one who defined himself as a jealous god. This meant they were unable to follow the normal practice of simply adopting Roman religious observances as a harmless veneer over their own personal beliefs. Instead they professed belief exclusively in their sole god, refusing to acknowledge any other possible source of divinity. This was obviously problematic when it came to worship of the emperor and, as a result, Jews found themselves marginalised within the Roman empire.

Some authorities tried to impose the Roman system on them through persecution, expelling them from Rome, destroying Jewish places of worship and introducing a Roman system of administration in Palestine. Palestine itself became a province of the Roman empire in AD 6, was renamed Judaea and was administered by a series of prefects. There was often tension between the Roman rulers and the Jewish people in this region and this came to a head in the First Jewish Revolt of AD 66. For a time the Jews tried to govern themselves by electing their own officials and issuing their own coinage, but in AD 70 the emperor Vespasian and his son Titus quashed this revolt and marked their victory by burning the temple of Jerusalem. Problems arose a second time between AD 115-118 in response to the emperor Trajan's attempt to prohibit circumcision, a cornerstone of Jewish identity.

In Rome itself during the reign of Tiberius (AD 14-37) Jews came in for increased suspicion and scrutiny from the authorities as a result of a financial scandal involving the alleged embezzlement of gifts intended for the temple at Jerusalem. Jews and Egyptians were dispatched from Rome to serve in the imperial army in Sardinia as a punishment for this perceived wrong; upwards of 4,000 of them were dealt with in this way (Tacitus, *Annals of Imperial Rome* 2.85). The emperor Claudius (*r.* AD 41-54) introduced a temporary ban on Jewish assemblies in another period of persecution (Suetonius, *Claudius* 25). Other Roman authorities, however, simply left the Jewish people in their community to their own devices; it was not until the reign of Septimius Severus (AD 193-211) that legislation was passed against actually converting to Judaism. The Jewish people were not interested in winning converts in the same way as Christians were. Judaism was not a proselytising religion. Authorities, therefore, were more disturbed by the 'un-Roman' practices of the Jews than by any threat of mass conversion. Many members of the Jewish community in Rome were also shrewd business people and therefore of use to the upper class citizens of Rome who could be profligate in their affairs. So, at worst in these cases, the Jews generally found themselves derided as stubborn and isolationist. They existed as a kind of sub-section of Roman society. Prior to the Christians, for example, the Jews were the first cult group to insist on separate burial grounds for their faithful and so Jewish cemeteries were kept distinct from Roman burial grounds.

Christianity, however, was a new departure because it was a proselytising religion. For the most part Jews had been content to be left alone; they did not try to impose their way of life on outsiders; they were inward-looking in this regard. Early Christians, on the other hand, felt themselves compelled to spread their new creed beyond their own community groupings, to bring it to the wider world. Since Christians were also monotheistic in their beliefs, their clash with Roman authorities was inevitable. What made it so acute was their insistence on proselytising; for this was read as a direct threat to the authority of the emperor and, even more worryingly, to the peace and prosperity of the Roman empire. This proved so much the case that in many quarters the perceived decline and fall of the empire has been laid at the door of the Christians and their new way of life.

It was, perhaps, an unfortunate coincidence that the continued expansion of the Christian Church came at a time when the empire itself was experiencing difficulties on a number of levels. Its sheer size led to all sorts of administrative difficulties, chief among which was the protection of its borders against outsiders or barbarians. Obviously, the greater the size of the empire and the longer the borders needing to be policed, the more inevitable it became that gaps would occur here and there along the line. So the citizens of the empire in those areas began to feel themselves stretched, as they nervously waited for the day when Roman military might would no longer be enough to protect them from those who wished to make their territory a target.

There were also financial constraints during this period, as emperors struggled to pay for the armies necessary to guarantee the empire's security and for the constant improvements in infrastructure essential for the administration of so large an empire. Most often, these funds were raised by taxing the citizens, sometimes leaving districts impoverished and their residents resentful. There were also the usual issues raised by succession to the imperial throne. It was rare that an emperor had a son or family member to whom power automatically passed on his death. The infamous Commodus was one of the very few imperial sons who had been groomed for succession from the time of his birth – contrary to the recent Hollywood portrait (in *Gladiator*) of a man disinherited by his own father in favour of the senate and a favourite general. Yet even an inherited emperorship was no guarantee of security; coups and usurpations became commonplace and recurring motifs of this period of Roman history. Emperors were removed because they were disliked by their subjects, because they had other, more powerful rivals or simply because they died early, either in battle or worn out with the effort of maintaining some semblance of order and prosperity throughout the empire. The emperor Geta, for example, reigned first with his father, Septimius Severus, between AD 209-211; but when he shared his reign with his brother Caracalla, from 211 onwards, he lasted less than a year before Caracalla had him murdered, so he could wield power alone. Another member of the Severan dynasty, Elagabalus (AD 218-222), was murdered and replaced at the instigation of the senate and the praetorian guard, who grew increasingly disgusted at his debauched style of living and his wilful manner of selecting officials. Between AD 238 and 284 some twenty emperors held office during a period that is described by some historians as 'fifty years of military anarchy', troops regularly taking it upon themselves to proclaim emperors and stage coups.

These difficulties increased during the second and third centuries AD, culminating in what is described by many ancient historians as 'the third century crisis'. Civil strife was endemic, the currency was constantly devalued and the spectre of barbarian hordes was familiar to every border outpost. There were some who sought scapegoats on whom to blame their hardships and anxieties. The Christians seemed an obvious choice, since they were entirely open about their refusal to acknowledge the emperor as deity. Their refusal was, in turn, interpreted as a wilful snub to the prosperity of the empire as a whole. As we have seen, traditional Roman religion was regarded as a public demonstration of allegiance to both emperor and empire as a means of safeguarding its continued success. A failure to observe these practices – and a failure that was as stubborn and obvious as that of the Christians – made it easy for some to draw connections between Christian defiance and localised social difficulties.

It has to be said that to speak of the third century AD as a period of crisis may be something of an exaggeration. The empire was *not* on the point of collapse: indeed the Mediterranean peoples had been so completely Romanised that it was hard to conceive of any other way of life or any other source of authority. Those who lived in North Africa or in Syria were just as likely to consider themselves Romans as those who lived in Italy or in the city of Rome itself. Nevertheless, similar difficulties were experienced by many of these citizens across the territory; so scapegoats were still sought. Some could feel justified in laying all the trials and tribulations of the Roman empire at the door of the Christians.

Christians and their beliefs had been used as explanations for Roman difficulties many years before the third century, however. The most infamous of these occasions was in AD 64 after the great fire of Rome, when the emperor Nero chose to accuse Christians of playing a part in that spectacular act of arson. The fact that the emperor himself was probably responsible for the fire is almost beside the point. The real issue was that Christianity had already spread sufficiently within society for its faithful to exist as a recognisably distinct group – and for outsiders to be suspicious of their behaviour and their motives. It was that latent suspicion which Nero exploited when he decided to denounce them publicly as responsible for the fire which had devastated so large an area of Rome.

Christian characteristics

What had enabled the Christians to gain such a firm a foothold in the capital of the empire so soon after the posited date for the death of Jesus? Edward Gibbon provided a summary of the factors he considered important, including among them what he called the 'inflexible, and if we may use the expression, the intolerant zeal of the Christians, the miracles performed by and on behalf of the faithful, and their "pure and austere morals"' (*The Decline and Fall of the Roman Empire*, ch. 8).

Certainly Christianity defined itself as a proselytising religion, intent on winning to the faith – and thus to salvation – as many converts as possible. This made for very public preaching in the faith's early days; and for a demonstrable style of living that was supposed to encapsulate all the Christian values. This is, in fact, one of the key aspects of early Christianity – that it was noticeably 'different' from other religions around it. While the Romans asked only that citizens perform the religious rituals appropriate to perpetuating the Roman way of life, Christians felt that *every* aspect of one's life should be altered by a commitment to their religion. Indeed early Christians were horrified that a member of the faithful might simply fade into the background of Roman society; they insisted instead on an open and obvious declaration of belief, through dress, religious ritual and even daily behaviour. It was therefore easy for suspicious neighbours to recognise the Christians in their midst – and to denounce them if they saw fit. And indeed many aspects of Christian behaviour must have been felt disturbing and threatening to the average Roman citizen.

In the first place, Christians professed that the kingdom of heaven was very much at hand, that it was time for believers to cast aside the things of this world if they were to be redeemed. This led to an ostensible disregard for material matters: hence the simple dress that many of them adopted, their insistence on giving alms and their disinclination for any of the normal activities of the Roman citizen. Christians did not approve of attendance at public games or theatrical events; for reasons already obvious, they did not partake in traditional religious rituals; and the most devout among them did not even work to accumulate wealth for future generations. All of these activities were intrinsic to the Roman way of life; they were part of its character. Christian difference in rejecting these practices only compounded their isolation from their contemporaries. Their way of life seemed not only different but also an outright threat to Roman traditions. If this distaste for customary civic activities, such as attending entertainments and religious festivals, were to continue, if the Christians' approach to material wealth were to take over in society, then everything that defined the Roman city and its success would be called into question and could conceivably collapse. So it becomes easier to see why a group of people espousing such an ostensibly peaceful and even beneficial philosophy should suddenly come to be regarded, quite literally, as enemies of the state.

Nero was apparently the first – and the most powerful – individual to tap into this growing unease with the Christian philosophy. Begun for his own malign ends, this first 'organised' persecution of the early Church lasted a number of years and provided the Christians with two of their most powerful martyrs – Peter and Paul. We know little about the death of Paul beyond the fact that he was imprisoned in Rome for a considerable time; a number of his epistles were written from his jail cell. He was accused by Jewish authorities of bringing gentiles into the Temple. It was customary for Roman citizens, of whom Paul was one, to be tried in Rome; hence his transfer to the capital city of the empire prior to his execution. There is only a little more detail available regarding the death of Peter. He too preached and wrote letters from Rome in these formative years of the Church. He was arrested and crucified, probably in the gardens of Nero along with many other Christians caught up in this wave of persecution. We are told that he was crucified with his head facing downwards, allegedly because he did not consider himself worthy to echo the position of the crucified Christ (Eusebius, *Ecclesiastical History* 2.1).

The persecution in which these prominent Church figures died would not have been possible had the Christians themselves not been so zealous – and therefore unpopular – in their proclamation of a new way of life and their even more disturbing insistence that the end was nigh. This sense of an imminent end, to be followed by a day of judgement and redemption, is itself a key to the fervour with which the early Christians behaved. A sense of urgency had been created and fostered in the early Church, leading to a very real belief that Christ's second coming was only a matter of years away. Jesus himself had promised to return and gather his disciples to him. He had warned that no one would know the day nor the hour. It was perhaps easier, therefore, for the faithful to be comfortable with the idea of casting aside the traditional comforts of life in the Roman empire in order to safeguard more eternal salvation – to be continually ready to face the final judgement.

Even more powerful to the early Christians than a rigorous cleansing of their lives, however, was the notion of dying for their faith, just as Jesus himself might be said to have done. This was seen as a sure and certain guarantee of salvation; so it was something that seems to have taken a strong hold of the Christian imagination. It is also an important factor when considering the early martyrs: not only did the climate of distrust, dislike and persecution create the opportunity for martyrdom but Christians themselves seemed to have had an almost romantic attachment to the concept. So dramatic personalities emerged into the limelight by virtue of their exceptionally gruesome deaths.

Chapter 2

Periods of Persecution

The Persecutions of Nero

From the time in AD 64 when Nero was able to rouse public discontent against the Christians, thus instigating the first 'official' persecution of the religion and its believers, Christianity enjoyed a mixed relationship with the Roman authorities until its legitimation by Constantine in AD 312.

Nero had been acting largely out of self-interest. The population of the city of Rome was clamouring for some form of justice after the great fire and, whether Nero was himself to blame for the conflagration or not, he evidently feared that, if he did not present the population with a culprit, they might be tempted to look to him for gratification instead. Since Christians were already somewhat suspect, it was easy to elevate them to the level of scapegoats, especially since few people had an accurate idea of what their creed entailed or what comprised their religious rituals. There was ample space for malicious rumour and accusation; Christians were quickly denounced as dangerous elements within society.

Either wilfully or as a result of sheer ignorance, the Romans levelled allegations of incest, cannibalism and sexual promiscuity against Christians. They wrote about the Christian habit of calling each other brothers and sisters and of greeting each other with kisses. This alluded to the Christian form of address by which they greeted each other as 'brothers and sisters in Christ' and may have offered as part of their greeting a ritual kiss of peace. Romans preferred to interpret the practices as indications of incest and sexual immorality. Pagans spoke of sinister rituals, held in secret locations, which they called 'love feasts'. Again this seems to be wilful misinterpretation of the Eucharist and its import as a rite of love. Christians would have been referring to the love of Christ and their love of each other as part of this ceremony but pagans preferred to believe that such rites were in reality orgies. Since Christians called each other brother and sister, then participated in such gatherings, they could only be guilty of incest. Finally, the central aspect of such a feast or ceremony was the eating of 'flesh' and the drinking of 'blood', Christians believing that they were partaking in the body and blood of Jesus Christ. To the Romans that was simply cannibalism; and, to support their claims, further rumours were spread to the effect that, during these feasts, Christians devoured small infants, which they had stolen from pagan households. With such a catalogue of crimes and misdemeanours, it is scarcely surprising that public opinion was swayed against the Christians with relative ease. So Nero had his scapegoats.[7]

His persecution of the Christians was gruesome indeed. They were rounded up – some denounced even by their neighbours or their own household slaves – and put to death. Some were hung on crosses and lit as torches throughout Nero's gardens. Others, the historian Tacitus tells us, were dressed in animal skins and thrown in this fashion to the city's stray dogs to be torn apart. It is interesting that, in spite of public dissatisfaction with the situation after the great fire and in spite of the need to blame someone, Tacitus reports that Christian victims of such brutality were in fact pitied by many of the Romans, since it was felt that their deaths served only Nero's depraved interests rather than the good of the city as a whole (Tacitus, *Annals of Imperial Rome* 15.43).

It is also worth noting here that, though arrested and executed as guilty of arson, Christians often faced another charge, invoked to justify their deaths. They were accused of 'anti-social tendencies' – a phrase that neatly summed up public perception of their isolation from the rest of the Roman population. Their insistence on keeping apart from traditional Roman rituals meant they held themselves separate from the very activities that would have defined them as upright Roman citizens. Instead they seemed to have no interest in acting as such and that naturally left their contemporaries anxious. Christians were not just isolationist;

they could in fact be endangering society itself by their refusal to participate in the rituals that safeguarded it – something that would have seemed most anti-social to the ordinary Roman observer.[8]

Trajan and Pliny: a blueprint for persecution

Once Nero's reign ended, however, outrage against the Christian Church subsided. It flared again only sporadically over the next decades. In many cases Christian persecutions were localised affairs – taking place in provincial towns and villages where practising Christians had deliberately marked themselves out as different from their fellow citizens. If ever trouble arose, whether through a poor harvest, an earthquake or some other natural calamity, it was often easiest to assume that the correct rituals to propitiate the appropriate gods had not been carried out and that the omission must be the fault of the obdurate Christians. However, there were no 'official' procedures for dealing with these issues: local authorities were generally left to deal with matters as best they could.[9]

A correspondence between Pliny the Younger (*Letters* 10.96 and 97) and the emperor Trajan provides an excellent illustration of the *ad hoc* methods used to persecute Christians. At the same time it also demonstrates the extent to which the religion had spread even to more out of the way provinces within the empire. The dates of Trajan's rule (AD 98–117) show just how rapidly Christianity had been disseminated, how soon it had recovered from Nero's persecutions – marks of its ability to survive and to win new converts.

Around AD 110 Pliny wrote to Trajan from his province of Pontus-Bithynia, a mountainous region at the very edges of the empire, on the southern coast of the Black Sea. In his capacity as governor Pliny was required to pass judgement on a variety of criminal and legal cases within his jurisdiction. It so happened that he was asked to adjudicate on the matter of some Christians who had been accused and brought before him. Pliny claims he has no notion as to the correct way to proceed, since he had 'never taken part in a trial of Christians'. He writes seeking the emperor's guidance. The letter carries the implication that trials of Christians may have grown relatively widespread at this time, though not so widespread that any central policy had been laid down in order to guide far-flung officials. Like others, Pliny was forced to act on his own initiative in this regard. He seems to have been relatively cautious. He is uneasy about the fact that those accused of being Christians could be drawn from any walk or stage of life. They could be young or old, female as well as male. Pliny instinctively feels that there are gradations and distinctions of punishment required in such a situation. He has, therefore, taken to conducting his own examinations of the accused brought before him. If they confess to being Christians and maintain this stance even after a second and third questioning, Pliny has no compunction in executing them, since they have, at any rate, demonstrated themselves more obstinate and recalcitrant than any member of a subject population ought to be. Those who possess Roman citizenship – still a carefully guarded and limited privilege in those days – are to be sent (like Paul before) to Rome for trial.

The granting of Roman citizenship was often used to absorb and placate the populations of the provinces as they became part of the ever expanding empire. Citizens of Rome had the right to vote for the magistrates who would administer the empire and also to serve as these magistrates if they were of suitable social and financial standing. Citizens were also liable for military service in the armies of the empire. They had a favourable tax status and were entitled to a full and fair trial if ever accused of a crime, whereas non-citizens could be prosecuted and punished at the whim of a local governor; citizens were entitled to be transported to Rome for their trial. Only certain punishments were suitable for a Roman citizen: flogging, for example, was not permitted, as the person of a Roman citizen was held to be inviolable. As such, citizenship was prized among the peoples and tribes annexed by the empire and there are numerous occasions in Roman history in which it was granted to entire social groups as a reward for loyalty or to prevent unrest, although its lofty status was steadily eroded as time went on and more and more people qualified for inclusion in the ranks of citizens. In AD 212 the emperor Caracalla decided to make the right of citizenship available to all free inhabitants of the Roman empire. This encompassed a vast population; people who lived at huge distances from Rome and who might never even have seen the city were nevertheless accorded citizenship of an empire that was administered from there, along with all the accompanying privileges. It is thought that there were no longer as many benefits as previously to being a citizen; certainly its free availability under Caracalla would have done much to remove the gloss of exclusivity. His edict simply offered legal recognition to the state of affairs whereby the expansion and Romanisation of the empire had made the majority of the free population in the Mediterranean world *de facto* Romans.

To return to Pliny's correspondence with Trajan, however; he seems to be faced with ever increasing numbers of accused, many of them apparently informed on unjustly. Perhaps some of the petty rivalries and jealousies endemic in any community were responsible for the denunciations. If someone appeared to be wealthier than his neighbour, if he had a better harvest or if he got the better of a business deal, jealousy could flare, along with a desire for revenge. There is anecdotal evidence from the Second World War to suggest something similar: that many of those who were imprisoned and executed by the Third Reich had been turned in by their neighbours, often for crimes no greater than that of being 'different'. Those who denounced them thought no further than their desire to rid the neighbourhood of a potentially disruptive influence; they did not expect the brutality and severity of the subsequent punishments. It would seem that something similar happened during periods of persecution endured by Christians. Pliny notices that often there seems to be little by way of concrete evidence against many of those denounced to him.

He has no intention of rendering so many people to summary execution. He asks each one to make a statement of religious commitment to Rome and her traditions. Once they deny that they are – or indeed ever have been – Christians, he requires that they make a sacrifice to the image of the emperor, as proof of their allegiance to Rome and its structures. He also asks them to curse Christ, out of a belief that no Christians could bring themselves to do such a thing. With these requirements answered, Pliny is happy to release them. He treats lapsed Christians similarly, after questioning them in an effort to understand what being a Christian actually entailed. All he manages to find out, however, is that they used to meet on a fixed day at dawn for the singing of verses to Christ, that they undertook to live virtuous lives, 'that they should not commit theft, robbery or adultery, that they should not break contracts, and that they should return money entrusted to them when called upon'. Even when he puts two slave women to a more rigorous interrogation – slave testimony was only considered reliable if taken under torture – Pliny can only uncover evidence of what he calls a *superstitio* – a 'trivial' set of beliefs, somewhat akin to what we would dismiss as 'superstition' today.

Trajan's answer to Pliny's detailing of events is in many ways the first 'official' response as to how Christians should be treated within the Roman empire. He commends Pliny for his actions to date and says that there should be no 'witch-hunt' for Christians. He is also happy to accept a sacrifice to his own image as sufficient proof of allegiance to Rome and to her religious rituals. This method of 'proof' became adopted by many other Roman authorities and we will see it recurring on a number of occasions in subsequent periods of persecution.[10]

Between Trajan and Diocletian

While it is impossible to state that Christians were not persecuted between the time of Pliny's letter and AD 170, we have no records that suggest any kind of large scale action against the religion or its followers. It is probably safe to assume that localised denunciations and prosecutions occurred, perhaps prompted by jealous citizens or disgruntled officials rather than any official edict from Rome. In many ways, Trajan's reply to Pliny in 110 seems to reflect the views of many authorities, and is even echoed by the emperor Hadrian in 123 when writing to a proconsul at Ephesus who found himself in a similar situation (Eusebius, *Ecclesiastical History* 4.8.6-9). So no concerted attempt was made to halt the spread of Christianity. It was only if Christians began to impede the life of a community in some obvious way that action had to be taken.

We know, however, that some Christians were martyred in these years and that their execution resulted from their adherence to the faith in spite of official disapproval. They were targeted as individuals who had fallen foul of their local authorities, rather than as part of any cohesive move against the Church. Little was done to identify or police Christian places of worship or monitor the rituals of their meetings. And it has to be borne in mind that Christians who were identified, then tried and executed, may have been denounced for reasons other than religious belief, perhaps even as a result of personal vendettas within their community. Officials had to be willing to follow up on any accusation levelled against alleged Christians; and evidence suggests that many of these officials were more cautious – even more apathetic – than our accounts of gruesome persecutions might lead us to believe. Those who think in terms of centuries of harsh and unrelenting persecution carried out against Christian communities do not present a historically accurate picture, rather a sense or a mood of oppression that best suits their aim to provide a continuous account of the Church triumphant. On the most practical level, blanket persecution cannot have occurred: had it done so, the attractions of the Christian religion would have been far outweighed by the dangers of conversion; the religion would probably never have progressed beyond minor cult status.

We do, however, have a number of martyr texts dating from AD 170 onwards and they indicate that this seems to have been a particularly fraught time for Christians.[11] In the reign of Marcus Aurelius we hear of new edicts against Christians in Asia, though this move does not necessarily seem to have been sanctioned by the emperor himself. Indeed it would have been somewhat at odds with Marcus' presentation of himself as a philosopher emperor to be so eager to rout out alternative beliefs and philosophies with such harshness. It is more likely that certain governors within the Asian provinces displayed a willingness to entertain anti-Christian allegations. Such persecutions were probably more often than not entirely local affairs, dependent on the temperament or even mood of the ranking official and on the extent to which he could be encouraged to take action by specific local interests-groups. This is a natural development, given the size of the empire; not every decision could always be presented to the emperor for approval.

There are also suggestions – though difficult to verify – that the Senate issued a decree against Christians in the 180s; and that in the mid 230s the emperor Maximinus issued an order against Church leaders. Scholars have subsequently decided that neither of these 'occasions' of persecution is by any means certain; so we are left with the probability that intermittent action against the Church and its followers may have been more often instigated by local magistrates than by edicts deriving from the emperor of the day.[12]

We come to a more definite time of anti-Christian action in AD 249-50 under the rule of Decius. This emperor issued an edict requiring all inhabitants of the empire to offer sacrifice to the gods and to obtain a certificate declaring that they had obeyed the decree. In fairness to Decius, the edict was more probably an attempt to bolster piety and civic feeling throughout the empire than a specific move against Christians. It failed to specify which gods had to be honoured, thus leaving the way open for people to sacrifice to their own local gods. Christians would not necessarily have needed to come into conflict with the traditional Roman gods; they could comply with the edict, provided they were ready to name their god as a local deity whom they worshipped in addition to the Roman pantheon. Nevertheless, the sacrificial requirement meant that those professing to be Christian could not conform *and* keep a clear conscience; for conformity would mean they had to acknowledge the existence of other deities; the practice of animal sacrifice would also run counter to Christian *mores*. Finally the necessity of providing a sworn affidavit would mean that they could not easily find a way around the proscription:

To those chosen to superintend the sacrifices in the village of
Alexander's Island; from Aurelius Diogenes, son of Sabatus,
of the village of Alexander's Island, aged seventy-two, with
a scar on his right eyebrow. I have always sacrificed to the
gods; and now in your presence in accordance with the terms
of the edict, I have sacrificed and have tasted the sacrificial
victims. I request you to certify this. Farewell. I, Aurelius
Diogenes have presented this petition.
   Witness: I, Aurelius Syrus, saw you and your son sacrificing.

(Inscription, cited in M. Beard, J. North & S. Price (eds),
Religions of Rome [CUP 1998] vol. 2, 6.8c).

It seems logical to suppose that most of those actually expected to
acquire such a certificate had in some way been connected with
Christianity. Otherwise we would have to accept that the administrative infrastructure of the empire was capable of witnessing a
sacrifice on the part of every single member of the population – *and*
of churning out the incredible number of legal documents required.
It is more probable that only those suspected of belonging to the
Christian community were asked to provide such direct proof of
their piety and allegiance to traditional Roman systems. It is hardly
surprising that a brisk trade in forged and illegal certificates grew
up around the empire; in many cases, it seems, Christian citizens
sent their slaves to sacrifice and obtain a certificate, which was
then used to clear the entire household of any accusation of
disobedience.

   It also appears that many Christians simply went into hiding to
avoid performing a public sacrifice or having to refuse to do so.
Even some church leaders may have done this, perhaps rational-
ising it with the belief that, if *they* were caught and executed,
their communities would have been unable to withstand further
persecution. Within the Church this gave rise to a new problem
– apostasy.

Lapsing and apostatising Christians

Willingness to suffer and die for the Christian faith became elevated to represent the ideal form of devotion and those who demonstrated reluctance might find themselves vilified by their more stalwart brethren. In some quarters those who opted to hide and wait for their local version of persecution to pass were regarded as 'incomplete' Christians; but severest censure was reserved for those who performed sacrifice to the Roman gods and obtained a certificate of compliance. In some cases Church authorities drew a distinction between those who simply purchased the certificate from some source in order to safeguard their family and those who actually performed the necessary sacrifices. Cyprian of Carthage (AD 200-258) was one such bishop, who was well aware that worldly concerns often constrained the Christians in his care, making them reluctant to face death for more esoteric reasons.[13] Indeed wealthy Christians seem to have been particularly at risk of persecution, both because of their visible place within the community and because their property, if they were convicted, became confiscate to the state. Many of them obtained the all-important certificate, either through bribery or through what their church leaders regarded as apostasy. Not everyone was as lenient as Cyprian, however, and his understanding approach toward his flock may have had much to do with the fact that he himself spent this period of persecution in hiding. In his efforts to regain their respect afterwards, he took a stricter line in his preaching, believing that those who had performed the pagan sacrifice to safeguard their lives had none of the Holy Spirit in them and were therefore unfit to either receive or administer the sacraments. However he always held out the hope of ultimate forgiveness and reconciliation with the body of the Church – something other authorities were less willing to allow.

Other leaders declared such Christians to be apostates and excommunicated them from the Church. And so seeds of division were sown. Over the next decades various factions emerged within the Church, some of which refused to re-acknowledge apostates, while others took a more lenient view, readmitting 'lapsed' Christians after a period of penance.[14] North African churches were often more severe and some of the best known Christian martyrs came from these communities, with their higher standards of what constituted Christian behaviour. It has been suggested that there was a tradition of self-sacrifice and willingness to die for a cause in Carthinginian history (Carthage was the principal city of North Africa at this time and the most cultured city of the empire next to Rome). The legendary founder of the city, Dido, was enshrined as the noble queen who committed suicide in the despair of unrequited love. It seems that large scale child sacrifices to the god Baal-Hammon were made at key crisis points in the city's existence in order to ensure its continued prosperity. In the Third Punic War the defeated Carthiginian general, Hasdrubal, was reviled for surrendering to the Romans, while his wife was admired for cursing him, killing their children, throwing them into the flames consuming the city and hurling herself after them.[15] A willingness to be martyred for adherence to the Christian faith may be a natural follow-on from this long and dramatic tradition; yet it would also serve as a reason for the lack of tolerance for those less willing to immolate themselves and the subsequent schismatic churches that emerged, each believing themselves more righteous and more truly Christian than those who had gone before. Such severe sects themselves came to be regarded as splinter groups from what became recognised as the true church, giving their names to some of the prominent 'heresies' of the day, such as the Donatists.[16]

The Donatists became divided from the main Catholic church of North Africa because of their attitudes to clergy who had surrendered the scriptures as commanded in the persecutions under Diocletian (AD 303-5). The Donatists branded these priests and bishops as traitors, claiming to be following the teachings of Tertullian and Cyprian. They refused to readmit such 'surrenderers' to their church and held them incapable of performing the sacraments. As a church, Donatism gained widespread currency in North Africa and a tenuous foothold in Rome itself but was denounced as heretical elsewhere. It was a comparatively long-lived schismatic church, however, since St. Augustine was still trying to reason with local Donatists in Thagaste, North Africa in AD 411. They seem to have declined in numbers and influence from about 412 onwards, when the emperor Honorius instigated a series of fines and legislation against them as an illegal sect.

To return to the period of 'state-sponsored' persecution under Decius: it has to be said that many Roman officials were loath to carry out numerous trials and executions purely on grounds of failure to offer sacrifice. In texts that detail the deaths of martyrs we read of repeated attempts on the part of governors and magistrates to get Christians to perform the sacrifice or to rethink their obstinate professions of faith. Some asked those brought before them whether they could not bring themselves simply to offer a pinch of incense to the gods, if animal-sacrifice was such anathema; and there must have been many who urged the accused simply to say the words of the oath and keep their feelings of faith private – in very much the way Roman religious rites were carried out. The Christians we hear about, however, refused all forms of compromise; they even persisted in arguing theology with the magistrates, trying to win converts even as they themselves faced death. Other Christians seem to have willingly placed themselves in the path of their persecutors.

There is one particularly striking story of a group of Christians who heard that a notoriously harsh governor was due to make a tour of their city. They presented themselves in front of his court, declaring themselves Christian and clamouring to be taken away and executed because of their religious beliefs (Tertullian, *Epistle to Scapula* ch. 5).[17] This governor was only too happy to oblige, though even he wondered what would happen if everyone who professed to be Christian demonstrated similarly 'suicidal' tendencies. Something of an atmosphere of hysteria seems to have been generated around the persecutions, prompting extreme actions by would-be martyrs. We hear of Christians who were moved to proclaim their own commitment to the faith simply by observing the courage displayed by their brethren on trial or in the arena – even if they themselves had been in no danger of persecution:

A whole squad of soldiers ... with an old man, Theophilus, were standing in court. When a man accused of being a Christian was on the point of denying Christ, they ground their teeth as they stood there, grimaced, stretched out their hands and gestured with their bodies. All eyes were turned towards them, but before anyone could stop them, they made a dash for the dock, saying that they were Christians. The governor and his fellow judges were filled with alarm; in contrast to the panic on the bench, the accused all showed a complete disregard of the sufferings to come; they marched out of the court in triumph ... their fame gloriously spread abroad by God.

(Eusebius, *Ecclesisastical History* 6.41.2; persecutions at Alexandria in the reign of Decius)

Caught up in the atmosphere of group-protest, some even called to be executed along with friends or family. Eusebius, the Church historian, himself witnessed some of these events during the persecutions under Diocletian through which he lived:

All the time I observed a most wonderful eagerness and a truly divine power and enthusiasm in those who had put their trust in Christ. No sooner had the first batch been sentenced, than others from every side would jump onto the platform in front of the judge and proclaim themselves Christians. They paid no heed to torture in all its terrifying forms, but undaunted spoke boldly of their devotion to God and with joy, laughter and gaiety received the final sentence of death.

(*Ecclesiastical History* 8.9.6)

It is hard today to conceive what may have motivated them, though there is evidence from more recent history to indicate the power of the group and the way in which people can be led to modes of behaviour that seem incomprehensible to a detached observer: we need only remember those in Nazi Germany who found themselves caught up in the general enthusiasm for a new order, despite the criminal actions that were part of the order; and the current rise in numbers of those drawn from various religions and ethnic groupings who are prepared to 'martyr' themselves for political ends by carrying out suicide terrorist attacks shows that the appeal of martyrdom has by no means diminished.

There were also theological reasons offered as inducement to early Christians facing persecution. A willingness to give up one's life for God was the ultimate expression of devotion – a sentiment actively encouraged by some of the early church fathers, who spoke of the heavenly glories awaiting those who died in this way and taught that martyrdom actually worked to erase all previous sins and wrongdoings, allowing the martyr to proceed directly to paradise, by-passing the usual judgement and atonement procedures. A martyr could expect the full hundred percent of their heavenly reward, more ordinary mortals only something lower down the scale. This idea was further supported by martyr texts in which the protagonists proclaimed their confidence of joining Christ in heaven as soon as they had departed this life, even detailing what this life might be like in accounts of their visions or dreams. The idyllic pictures thus presented happily coincided with the feeling that this world would not last long into the future and added yet another factor to the mix that facilitated their dramatic declarations of faith.

The Decian persecutions were by no means the last faced by Christians, even though they had lost some of their bite by the end of the 250s. Decius himself was dead by 251 but there were others who carried on the spirit of the persecutions throughout the decade, among them the emperor Valerian (*r.* AD 253-260) who issued edicts forbidding Christians to meet for worship, singling out priests and bishops for execution. In AD 260-1, however, Gallienus issued a new edict granting peace and toleration to Christian churches throughout the empire. He even went so far as to restore some of the property earlier confiscated from them. A form of collaboration grew up in parts of the empire, whereby Christians were permitted silent observance of their own religious rituals, sometimes combined with civic duties in their local towns – in some cases even with municipal priesthoods. It has been suggested that the Roman authorities, being themselves preoccupied with far more immediate threats to the empire during this period, may have lacked the energy required for a consistent all-out persecution of Christians. The borders of empire were under constant pressure from barbarian invasions. Emperors frequently reigned for only two or three years; their chances of enforcing empire-wide policy changes with any degree of success were much curtailed.

The 'great persecution'

Yet in AD 303 another period of persecution began – this time under the emperor Diocletian. It has sometimes been labelled the 'great persecution'. Diocletian is the emperor whose actions are generally described as resolving the 'third-century crisis' – as we have seen, an exaggerated description of the instability plaguing the empire during the period. Barbarians continually threatened the frontiers. The Roman army now consisted of many cohorts which had themselves once been considered barbarian but were now assimilated into the empire. There was always lingering suspicion about their loyalty; commanders and generals must have wondered what would happen if these troops were ever called upon to fight against their former compatriots. In addition, financial hardship struck many areas of the empire as emperors struggled to raise funds through increased taxation. The currency of Rome, which had once had a cachet similar to that of the American dollar in recent times, was steadily devalued over a period of decades. Administrative procedures crumbled in face of the distances between central command and the outlying provinces. There was a struggle to maintain the societal structures that would ensure continuous supply of food and wealth for the empire's larger cities. To speak of all this as a 'crisis', however, conveys a sense of sudden collapse in order and prosperity. In fact it was a more gradual process – and one which had differing degrees of severity in different locations. It is unlikely that many citizens of the empire ever felt themselves to be in the state of chaos or difficulty sometimes suggested by historians. It is indeed the system of sweeping reforms instigated by Diocletian on his accession to the throne in AD 284 that goes some way towards creating the notion of crisis. Diocletian's response to the inefficiencies of the empire now under his control was a radical alteration of its administrative structures, intended to have them run more smoothly. He also took steps to 'revalue' the currency; he reformed the tax system; and issues of defence came in for similar attention from this highly organised and organising emperor. Such a striking raft of changes, effected in a relatively short period, make it understandable that they are sometimes represented as responses to some clearly defined, immediate crisis. It may just have been that Diocletian was particularly gifted in administrative matters and acted accordingly. He was helped by the fact that his rule lasted considerably longer than that of many third-century emperors: he had the chance to enact reforms that may simply have been too time-consuming for some of his predecessors.

Part of Diocletian's reforms involved an attempt once again to get all citizens to sacrifice to the traditional gods and to curtail the activities of the Christians. In many ways the new round of persecutions seems to have arisen from a kind of superstition on the part of the emperor and his colleagues. When omens did not turn out positively from sacrifices, when reforms did not always proceed as smoothly as might have been wished, it was decided that Christians were somehow hindering the work of the emperor by imposing their religious practices in place of the rites and practices of more 'traditional' citizens. In one case it was thought that a ceremony did not ensure success for imperial endeavours precisely because a Christian present made the sign of the cross at the crucial moment. Such a reaction is perhaps understandable if we put ourselves in the shoes of the emperor and witness his struggle to reverse some of the misfortunes of his empire. We have already seen the extent to which Roman religion was bound up with perceptions of the health and prosperity of the empire. Any threat to that prosperity could easily be interpreted as though the traditional religion were somehow failing in its purpose. If Christians were found to be stubbornly refusing to take part in traditional Roman rites, then a ready made group of scapegoats existed on whom the authorities could vent their spleen.

As always the extent to which Diocletian's persecution was felt varied across the empire, depending on the region and on the authorities in question. Diocletian, as part of his administrative reforms, was the first emperor to make official what had become a practical division between the eastern and western halves of the empire. The division had a lot to do with linguistic differences but also with the sheer size of the territory involved. So we have the 'Greek East' and the 'Latin West' formally established for the first time in Roman history. To administer this new, bi-partite empire Diocletian took a colleague in the imperial purple: Diocletian himself ruled the east, leaving the affairs of the west to his partner Maximian. Both emperors also had junior assistants (or 'Caesars'), who became the intended successors to each imperial ruler. In this way the workload became more manageable; and, at the same time, the usually tricky problems of succession were solved – at least in theory. However, while Diocletian and his Caesar, Galerius, vigorously pursued their policy of persecution in the East, in the West things were much more relaxed. Maximian's Caesar, Constantius, contented himself with simply closing and destroying a few churches in his jurisdiction; no one was executed. And when Constantius died in AD 306, his army loyally proclaimed his son, Constantine (who was in York at the time), as the next emperor. Constantine's own Christian leanings will be discussed below; but they were at least sufficient to ensure that there was no further active persecution of Christians under his rule.

After Diocletian's retirement in AD 305, persecution of Christians was much more severe in the East. His successor, Galerius, seems to have been particularly enthusiastic in his efforts to restore traditional Roman piety. Martyr accounts dating from the period indicate widespread persecution and many horrible executions. Christians themselves take great pleasure from the fact that Galerius died in 311 after a revolting illness, which they saw as just punishment for his hostility toward the Church. The church-historian Eusebius does not stint in relaying the details:

> He was pursued by a divinely ordained punishment, which began with his flesh and went on to his soul. Without warning, suppurative inflammation broke out round the middle of his genitals, then a deep-seated fistular ulcer: these ate their way incurably into his inmost bowels. From them came a

teeming indescribable mass of worms, and a sickening smell
was given off; for the whole of his hulking body, thanks to
over-eating, had been transformed even before his illness
into a huge lump of flabby fat, which then decomposed
and presented those who came near with a revolting and
horrifying sight.   (Eusebius, *Ecclesiastical History* 16.1)

The writer is not surprised that Galerius, in such agony, 'was
filled with remorse for his cruel treatment of God's servants',
giving orders that the persecutions should be stopped. Indeed
he issued an edict to this effect, commanding tolerance among
all the peoples of the empire – and even the rebuilding of some
churches. Society was, however, slower to recant than Galerius;
even after his death in 311, there were still some requests from
various regions that the emperor deal with the Christians.
Maximin, Galerius' successor, was apparently eager to continue
the business of persecution but internal power struggles ensured
that his own rule was brief and in AD 312 Constantine emerged as
the chief power broker in the empire as a whole.

Chapter 3

The Language of Suffering and Death

The account of Galerius' final illness is interesting for both style and content. Clearly a Christian author, such as Eusebius, had no compunction about describing the gruesome detail of the disease. He even takes a kind of sneaking pleasure in its horror. We might think that this was because Galerius had been so brutal to Christians brought before him, that Eusebius was feeling a certain righteous anger. But such presentations of suffering were by no means confined to those of whom Christian authors disapproved. Throughout the many martyr texts that we have from the Church's various periods of persecution, there is a consistency in the way in which their tortures are presented in detail. In many ways it is a new genre of writing, whereby heroic deaths become all the more laudable if the sufferings preceding them have been demonstrably agonising. Roman audiences were, of course, no strangers to the concept of suffering, torture and death; much has already been written about their love of gladiatorial combat and the contests witnessed in the amphitheatre.[18] In many ways such events facilitated a kind of *katharsis* on the part of the audience: they could vent their anger or their distress through vicarious experience of the thrill of combat; similarly they could feel the power of life and death, albeit at a distance. Crowds attending such spectacles had an identity all their own: they embodied the entire community, with its raw desires, dislikes and enmities. The circus was a fitting outlet for such emotion, which could have been potentially lethal, had it been expressed outside the confines of the arena. Many emperors understood this all too well and were anxious to ensure that the 'mob' remained favourable to them, by affording them frequent and ample opportunities to indulge these emotions.

During the times of particularly harsh persecution, Christians often became the new gladiators. The crowds continued to treat their gruesome executions as both emotional outlet and entertainment. But what is most interesting is that the Christians themselves seemed to have followed suit, though with different aims. We have already seen how some Christians were so inspiring in their courage and defiance that they created a whole atmosphere of rebelliousness and daring around them, leading others to embrace trial and execution voluntarily, as they became caught up in the mood of the moment. In this respect, the emotional *katharsis* sparked in the martyrs themselves became very real – not at the remove of the audience at a conventional circus spectacle. The written accounts of these martyrdoms were also designed to create emotional responses in their readers. The authors may have hoped to inspire them by the events detailed in these texts to live more devout Christian lives, to ensure that their lifestyles became more obviously Christian against the back-drop of more traditional religious practices. Christianity was a religion that demanded a definite code of behaviour from its adherents – a code visibly manifested in their appearance, their actions and their daily priorities. It must obviously have been difficult in times of anxiety and persecution. We know that many Christians hid or toned down their observances to avoid detection and denunciation; but this was deeply disturbing to many Christian leaders, as can be seen from the schisms and factions that emerged within the church body. There were occasions when those who demonstrated such instincts for self-preservation suddenly found themselves branded as heretics, facing long periods of penance if they wished to be restored to the favour of the Church. Others managed to maintain a precarious balance between their Christian consciences and the demands of the civil authorities. For both groups the martyr texts served an important purpose – either to shame or to encourage them to better behaviour in their own lives.

It is for this reason that so many of the texts contain so much detail about the tortures and executions they describe. The more extreme the sufferings of martyred Christians, the more shaming it was that some who *claimed* to be faithful actually ran away and hid. Equally, the more extreme the martyrs' sufferings and the greater their defiance, the more encouraged ordinary Christians would be to follow assiduously the precepts of their religion. So most of the accounts of martyrs spend a great deal of time describing their cross-examination by intolerant pagan magistrates. It is an approach that allows the author to remind readers of the theological truths embraced by his heroes and heroines, to spur them to greater devotion. Yet it needs also to be added that there was a sheer entertainment value in these texts, facilitating their spread and their survival. Portraits of bravely defiant Christians facing down weak, ignorant governors themselves echoed the gladiatorial contests in which seemingly weaker opponents were pitched against heavily armed warriors. They evoked the spirit of the underdog, enlisting the support of readers on the side of the lesser combatant, quite irrespective of combatant's or readers' religious beliefs. Descriptions of imprisonment, torture and death served similar ends. Readers could experience martyrdoms at a remove, in just the way Roman audiences experienced armed combat and death at a distance while they sat cheering in the amphitheatre. There is even something of a salacious pleasure taken in the relation of gory details for readers' secret enjoyment. So many of the surviving texts do not stint on their descriptions of the terrible agonies suffered by martyrs before they died. They are grimly entertaining and effective at the same time.

In this way the martyr texts become a 'genre' of literature in their own right. They move beyond the simple recording of the events of the persecutions around the empire. They are sensational, idealistic and inspirational in equal measure; and they present a new brand of hero or heroine to the Roman audience.[19] One of the best known of these heroines is St. Perpetua and the account of her martyrdom sheds light not just on the way Christians viewed their martyrs but on the way Christians were perceived as a very real threat to the fabric of Roman society.

The martyrdom of St. Perpetua

Perpetua was a well-born young woman from the city of Carthage, a leading urban community in North Africa. In many ways her family seems to have been traditionally Roman, for all their

'African' location. Her father, as typical Roman *paterfamilias*, held ultimate power within the household. It was he who would have decided on matters of business, marriage, inheritance and succession. He would have been responsible for the obedience and civic virtue of his family. And all this would have been true even without the practice of Christianity. Somehow Perpetua came in contact with Christian influences and began to explore the religion actively.

One of the many sticks with which pagan authors beat Christianity was its appeal to women, slaves and inferior members of society. Since women were regarded as weaker and less intellectually able than men, their interest in converting was seen as an indictment of the religion itself – that it should be attractive to such a fickle and ineffectual sex. Nevertheless, the relationships between women in Roman households meant that it was often comparatively easy to spread the message of Christianity among them, winning converts that way rather than mounting a head-on assault upon the more traditional males. As women were held to have little power in the public sphere, it may have been that their private religious rituals and beliefs were not investigated too thoroughly by the *paterfamilias*, whereas the man of the household was of necessity a much more public figure. His religious observances must also have been largely public, directed at upholding the prosperity of household, community and state. Whatever the reasons, it was often through the female inhabitants that Christianity first entered a household; and it was in this way that some men came to be converted themselves.

Perpetua was one such woman; and one of her slave-women, Felicity, was also imprisoned and martyred along with her. These events took place in AD 203, too early for one of the persecutions of Christians sanctioned on an empire-wide basis. It seems that Perpetua and her fellow Christians in Carthage were unlucky enough to come to the attention of a particularly zealous magistrate, Publius Aelius Hilarianus, who felt so strongly about the importance of traditional Roman piety that he actively sought out and tried Christians. The most that the current emperor, Septimius Severus, had to say on the matter was that citizens were forbidden to convert to either Judaism or Christianity; but in Carthage the interpretation was more severe. The circumstances surrounding Perpetua's arrest are not clear but she was taken, along with her slave Felicity and several other of the community's Christians. What is unusual about Perpetua's martyr text is that much of it is ostensibly written in her own words, with just an anonymous 'top and tail' to give it context. At the very outset, therefore, there are a number of factors that would ensure the audience's interest: the protagonist is a young, wealthy woman, who would spark romantic interest; to add pathos, she has an infant son still at the breast; the body of the text is penned by the martyr herself; and she faces opposition not only from the severe magistrate but also from her own father. So Perpetua's martyrdom shows us the private, personal conflicts that may have been experienced by many of these Christians, as well as the more obvious, public confrontations with authority.

At the time of her arrest Perpetua was actually still a *catechumen* (a Christian under instruction, not yet baptised). This exaggerates the courage on her part, because she is willing to profess herself a Christian and to face the inevitable trial and execution, even though it would have been easier for her, unbaptised, to avoid her fate. She underwent baptism in prison; and there she was also allowed to have her infant son with her, alleviating the anxieties she had been experiencing. Her subsequent peace of mind allowed her to withstand the entreaties of her father, who had initially flown at her 'as if to pluck out my eyes' on hearing her profession of Christianity (*Martyrdoms of Sts Perpetua and Felicity* ch. 3). Concern – and normal fatherly feeling for the members of his household who had been imprisoned – softened his approach the next time they met. He appealed piteously to her to consider his grey head, his good name in society and the future of her own child (ch. 5). Perpetua had been strengthened, however, by a vision showing the heavenly glories that awaited her and her companions if they remain steadfast. Such pictures of paradise feature in many martyr texts, although here they are reported as visions that Perpetua requested and received from above in order to instil courage into the prisoners. With their minds fixed on this promised reward, the martyrs-elect became more and more detached from worldly concerns, enabling them to withstand the constant interrogation and the frequent demands to perform traditional Roman sacrifices. The visions also enabled

Perpetua to defy her father's wishes, even to ignore his appeals
to the natural bond between parent and daughter. This departure
from conventional feelings and emotions is apparent in Perpetua's
description of their sentencing at the hands of Hilarianus:

> Then Hilarianus passed sentence on all of us: we were con-
> demned to the beasts, and we returned to prison in high spirits.
>
> (ch. 6)

This gives us a glimpse of the communal mood of enthusiasm
enjoyed among the prisoners, enabling them to face their sentence
of death with comparative equanimity. The group dynamic fostered
a sense of optimism and willingness to sacrifice themselves
– something much harder for a lone individual to achieve.

Fortuitously, Perpetua's only barrier to this sense of detachment
dissolved: her infant suddenly weaned himself off the breast,
meaning that she no longer had to worry about breast-feeding
him or about how he would be cared for. Evidence that this
whole sequence of events must be God's will is found in the fact
that her breasts were not even inflamed or painful following so
sudden a cessation in breast feeding. Now Perpetua could devote
herself entirely to her fellow prisoners and to her visions, which
she recounts at length in her prison diary. In one of her visions
she saw herself stripped off in the arena, ready to do combat
with an Egyptian gladiator; and in this vision she appeared as a
man (ch. 10). This introduces us to a common Christian theme,
whereby virtuous women somehow transcend their sex through
willingness to suffer, thus becoming more like men. It is a telling
device, in that it demonstrates the inferior place of women in
public perception, as well as the Christian idea of their scope for
redemption. It is a kind of double standard that has often been
commented on by scholars of the period, who are frustrated by
the seemingly ineradicable misogynism of pagans and Christians
alike.[20] Yet Perpetua was so much a product of traditional Roman
society that she herself invokes the device without comment. Her
visions continued until the eve of her execution and, through them,
she kept up her own spirits and those of her comrades, buoyant
and secure in the knowledge that they would proceed directly to

the kingdom of heaven as a result of their deaths.

Felicity, too, managed to divorce herself from the traditional female role of mother as part of the same sequence of events. She had been pregnant at the time of her arrest and it was governmental policy to postpone executions of pregnant women until their child had been delivered, lest it be counted a double murder. Far from welcoming the reprieve, Felicity was horrified that she might have to face death separately from her companions. The reason given for her horror is her fear of being executed alongside common criminals rather than with fellow-Christians, though it may in fact have been a fear that in isolation from her comrades her enthusiasm for martyrdom might wane. Robbed of the group's support, it might have been more difficult for a young slave-woman to face her death in the arena bravely, before an audience unappreciative of the fact that her new faith had, in theory, granted her equality both with free citizens and with men. It is perhaps in recognition of the power of the group dynamic that Felicity's fellow prisoners combined in prayer to ensure she was delivered of her child just two days before they were due to die in the arena (ch. 14). The group cohesion was thereby maintained and they went together to their execution in a mood of mutual encouragement and support.

So confident were these martyrs of their salvation that they harangued the audience as they were herded into the arena, warning them that God would condemn the mob for their actions. The mob, therefore, clamoured for them to be scourged and we are told that the martyrs rejoiced at this; for it meant that they could have a share in the sufferings of Christ himself. The next part of the account, taken over by the anonymous narrator, details the ordeals of the various martyrs within the group. Some of the men were pitted against wild beasts; but such was their steadfastness that the animals were unable to harm them until such time as the Lord willed it. The women were to be thrown to a mad heifer – placed in nets to be tossed by it. In spite of being gored and trampled by the beast, Perpetua was more concerned with her modesty than her ordeal, displaying a dignity impressive even to the blood-thirsty mob – for a time. On being returned to the cells beneath the amphitheatre, she is described as awakening

from a kind of trance and asking when she was due to face the
ordeal of the heifer (ch. 20). Once again this is described as the
epitome of sanctity – that, so fixated on thoughts of Christ and
salvation, she failed even to notice that she had received such
a horrific mauling. It might, however, also be interpreted as the
brain's self-detachment from its surroundings as a mechanism to
cope with trauma and extreme pain. Throughout the martyr texts
we see divine explanations for actions that also have a physical or
mental logic behind them.

The presentation of the martyrs, rather than the mob or the magistrates, as the ones who held the power throughout is continued in
the description of the death of one of the group, Saturus, who had
declared that he would be killed by a single bite from a leopard;
and indeed it proved so – but only once he himself had announced
that the moment of his death had come (ch. 21). In this way
Christians are shown to have power even over dumb beasts by
reason of their virtue. Saturus then gave a ring soaked in his own
blood to the soldier who had been his guard, indicating the power
such relics would come to have in the future life of the Church.
Perpetua, too, could not be dispatched until she had declared her
willingness. It was as if their deaths were entirely voluntary rather
than the result of misguided persecution and bigotry. Perpetua was
lined up for decapitation but the executioner's first stroke went
astray; it was only when she reached up and steadied his hand that
she was finally killed:

> It was as though so great a woman, feared as she was by the
> unclean spirit, could not be dispatched unless she herself were
> willing.   (ch. 21)

Perpetua's martyrdom illustrates quite clearly the clash of
Christian and Roman ideals and the way in which that clash
could threaten the very foundation of Roman society. Contrary
to all expectations, Perpetua had disobeyed her father – the
head of her household – and, for doing so, she was regarded as
admirable by her biographer. When Christians lauded this kind
of behaviour, it is not surprising that the Romans came to regard
them with such suspicion and fear, since a threat to the order of

the household constituted a threat to the whole society. The threat was compounded by the fact that both Perpetua and Felicity were apparently ready to give up their infant children with little sign of distress, thus undermining the other main relationship within stable society – the bond between mother and child. With established ties torn asunder all round them in such a visible manner, it is small wonder that some of the crowd should have clamoured for the execution of these Christians, if only to gain some sense of order being restored.

The Christians saw themselves as proceeding according to Jesus' proclamation that those who loved him should leave behind their families and their earthly cares. The pagan members of Roman society, meantime, were witnessing a very real enactment of this esoteric declaration. The martyrdoms of Perpetua (and those like her), therefore, allowed pagans to observe the punishment for so destabilising society; and to exorcise in some way the demons to which it gave rise. The Christians were at the same time demonstrating a new spiritual equality between the sexes and between social classes that would also have been disturbing to its observers, who once again interpreted it more literally than even the Christians themselves. Perpetua would never have declared herself the equal of a man – except in the hour of her death and in her devotion to God. Similarly, Felicity would never have enjoyed the company of free-born citizens – except in such extenuating circumstances. But what the crowd saw were young women who acted as the equals of those whom society traditionally regarded as their superiors. This, too, sent a shock-wave through conservative Roman society.

Fascinating horror

Perpetua's martyr text is, as we have said, also interesting for its sheer 'entertainment value'. There is a kind of fascinated horror on the part of the readers as they focus on the ordeals suffered by each of the martyrs – an echo of what was felt by the audience in the arena itself. We are told that the audience were appalled at the sight of Perpetua and Felicity stripped naked, ready to be tossed by the mad heifer. Their horror arose from the fact that one was 'a delicate young girl and the other was a woman fresh from childbirth with the milk still dripping from her breasts' (ch. 20). The sight so displeased the public that the women were take out and brought back to the arena in unbelted tunics. There is a little about this passage that titillates while, at the same time, provoking disgust and revulsion. It brings to mind Plato's passage about the pull of 'appetite' over reason and the emotions, where he describes the automatic inclination on the part of the human beings to stop and stare at executed criminals, even as the heart and mind object to such voyeurism (*Republic* 5.2.440). It is the same phenomenon that today makes motorists slow down to 'rubber neck' a pile-up, even as they themselves feel horror at the thought of the carnage involved. Perhaps it is even a way of feeling a sense of well-being – their own luck in stark contrast to that of the victims. Thus Christian readers of such texts feel privileged that the martyrs involved have undergone such tortures on their behalf, while their baser instincts are somehow satisfied by the details of gore and agony.[21]

It is interesting to note that those martyr texts which have female martyrs as their main protagonists are often those that linger especially mawkishly on details of torture and endurance. This must have been a way of capitalising on the entertainment value of the events in order to hold the attention of the audience. It is almost as if the texts 'tease' their readers – offering tantalising glimpses of the horrific, without fulfilling the implied promise to reveal all. It makes the focus on the main characters all the more intense; and that must have suited authors who were trying to convey a sense of the heroism and sanctity of their protagonists. So, for example, some texts deal with women brought before magistrates and sentenced to detention in a brothel. In the account of the martyrdoms of Agape, Irene and Chione, which took place some time during the persecutions under Maximian (around AD 304 in Saloniki [Thessalonica] Macedonia), the prefect trying the case pronounced the following sentence on Irene:

> I sentence you to be placed naked in the brothel with the help of the public notaries of this city, and of Zosimus the executioner; and you will receive merely one loaf of bread from our residence, and the notaries will not allow you to leave ... Be it known to you that if ever I find out from the troops that this girl was removed from the spot where I have ordered her to be, even for a single instant, you will immediately be punished with the most extreme penalties.
>
> (chs 5-6)

The readers' voyeuristic side is immediately engaged by this account: how will Irene face the punishment? The 'teasing' nature of the text is quickly apparent when the author tells us that:

> ... by the grace of the Holy Spirit which preserved and guarded her pure and inviolate for the God who is the lord of all things, no man dared to approach her, or so much as tried to insult her in speech.much as tried to insult her in speech.
>
> (ch. 6)

It is a cunning approach: we are enlisted on the side of the martyr by imagining the terrible degradation and suffering decreed for her by the prefect but do not have to witness it or to consider the violation of one whom we are now asked to revere as a saint.

The martyrdom of Eulalia (pictured on the cover of this volume) is another text in which the reader is encouraged to gaze on the female body and its suffering but the final 'exposure' is denied at the last moment. Eulalia, a native of Merida in Spain, was martyred during the persecutions under Diocletian (AD 303-5), apparently at the tender age of twelve. Her martyr account is written by Prudentius (*Peristephanon* 3), who tells us of the girl's sweet nature, modesty and devotion. Eulalia was actually eager for martyrdom, hearing Diocletian's edict regarding sacrifice to the imperial gods as a call to battle. Her mother responded by forcibly removing Eulalia from the city to their country estate (*Peristephanon* 3.36-40). Eulalia, however, escaped from her vigilant parent and walked back to Merida in order to confront the governor and reproach him for his acts of persecution against the Christians. He ordered her to be arrested and then threatened her with instruments of torture in a bid to get her to perform the required sacrifice. He also reminded her of her good social standing and the grief her defiance would cause to her parents. The governor even tried to conjure up images of Eulalia as a bride and a mother in an effort to get her to turn aside from her rush to martyrdom. His expectations of a typical young female in Roman society are utterly confounded by her, however, and she deliberately and obviously turns aside from her conventional role, as demonstrated in her escape from her mother's protection. Eulalia spat at the governor on hearing his attempts to turn her from her faith and so was seized and tortured in the public forum. Prudentius describes the way in which soldiers used iron hooks to tear her sides and torches to burn her breasts (131-150). Although her body was naked and on show to the onlookers, Eulalia used her long hair to cover her nudity. Rather than groaning in pain, she gave constant thanks to God until such time as the smoke and flames engulfed her face and head. A white dove supposedly flew out of her mouth at the moment of her death (161-65), which so frightened her executioners that they abandoned the body and fled. Rather than leave her naked and tortured body exposed for all to gaze on, however, a snowfall covered over her nakedness thereby protecting her modesty even in death (176-80).

The very youthfulness of Eulalia is the most arresting aspect of this martyr account; it is the reason we focus so intensely on the protagonist. There is a certain titillating element to the description of her tortures and the display of her young body for her enemies – and the readers – to gaze on, emphasised by the dramatic way in which her torments are recorded. These are also placed in stark contrast to pictures of her as a dutiful daughter, wife or mother so that the audience are in no doubt as to the dramatic extent of her self-sacrifice. The promise of this teasing portrait of a stripped and tortured maiden is never fully delivered, however, as first her hair and then a snowfall, are used as barriers against those who would look inappropriately.

The account of the martyrs of Lyons is another text in which the gruesome sufferings of the victims are presented in considerable detail – both as a means of underlining the diabolical nature of the persecutors, and as a way of evoking this sense of fascinated horror among its readers. It is thought that these martyrs met their end in AD 177, during a localised period of persecution. In this instance the magistrates were probably responding to public opinion rather than any official statement of policy. Christians had become unpopular within Lyons (Roman *Lugdunum*); the people clamoured for their removal. The author speaks of two groups emerging from among the martyrs-elect. The first were those *eager* to face death for their faith, the second are described as weaker, untrained and unprepared to face such an ordeal. Some even recanted their professions of Christianity, presumably agreeing to swear whatever oaths of allegiance to the emperor and perform whatever sacrifices were required. Our author describes these failed martyrs as 'stillborn', alluding to the Christian belief that martyrs were reborn in Christ because of their sufferings. Even at this early stage, therefore, we see the roots of schism taking hold within the Church, some groups claiming superiority over others on grounds of their greater devotion, measured in terms of their ability to withstand suffering in defence of the faith. For them the greatest fear was, not that the suffering might be too terrible to endure, but that some of their number might lapse along the way (*Martyrs of Lyons* chs. 11-14).

Again in this account one of the most brutally tortured martyrs is a woman, Blandina, who was granted such power from God that she was able to endure maltreatment day and night – to the extent even of leaving her persecutors worn out and at the limits of their invention of fresh ways to coerce her into recantation. Like Perpetua, she is sometimes described as insensible to the pain (ch. 56) – interpreted by the author as a gift from God, though the phenomenon has been noted by modern psychologists as well. Blandina and other women among the group of martyrs are spoken of as triumphing over their naturally weaker nature; and the details given of their sufferings help underscore the author's surprise and admiration for their fortitude.

The text describes the sufferings of male martyrs as well; and there is some degree of the 'supernatural' in the account. Sanctus irritated the authorities by his constant reiteration of the response

'I am a Christian', even to questions about his citizen status. So they tried pressing red hot plates against the most tender parts of his body. A few days later they returned to torturing him, believing that his already damaged body would be unable to withstand further abuse and that he would recant. The opposite happened: his body actually recovered under the fresh round of torture; his bruises and wounds even disappeared (ch. 24). He and his companions were, nonetheless, sentenced to death in the arena and it is for this climax that the author reserves his most gruesome accounts of torture and suffering:

> Once again in the amphitheatre Maturus and Sanctus went through the whole gamut of suffering as though they had never experienced it at all before ... Once again they ran the gauntlet of whips, the mauling by animals, and anything else that the mad mob shouted for and demanded. And to crown all they were put in the iron seat, from which their roasted flesh filled the audience with its savour.   (chs 38-9)

Once Maturus and Sanctus have been dispatched in this way, Blandina takes centre stage again – this time hung on a post for wild beasts to maul. She is literally the focus for all eyes at this point, both those in the arena and those reading the text. She seems to the Christians as if hung in the form of a cross, reminding them of why they are suffering this way (ch. 41). The symbolism, combined with the mutual support of the group dynamic, ensures that many of them die enthusiastically. Yet, once again, the female body is preserved inviolate; none of the animals will touch Blandina; and she is returned to prison for another day. This pattern in which the female person is made object of the audience's gaze is worked out again and again in Christian writing. Quite literally, women like Blandina are reduced to objects, to be 'looked at', either symbolically by devout Christians or in stark reality by those actually observing the martyrdoms or reading the texts for entertainment.

Blandina returns to the arena after a few days' interval; meantime the Roman citizens accused of being Christian have been tried under rules different from those applicable to non-citizens. This time, Blandina is paired with a boy aged about fifteen. The mob are unmoved either by her womanhood or his youth. The author briefly surveys the torments endured by Blandina – the scourge, wild animals, a hot griddle, and being exposed to a bull. The brief mention made of each of these modes of torture seems to indicate that the readership would have been familiar with each blood-thirsty aspect of Roman spectacles. At any rate, Blandina eventually succumbs to them, although she has lost awareness of how she is being tortured 'because of the hope and possession of all she believed in and because of her intimacy with Christ'.

This text does not simply end, as most others do, with the death of the leading martyrs. Instead the mob are portrayed as inflamed by the Devil and prompted by him to deny the martyrs proper burial. The corpses are thrown to the dogs and left unburied for up to six days. Then they are burned and the ashes swept into the river so that no relics of them would remain. Even in the second century, therefore, it seems that there was already awareness of the kind of cults that could grow up around Christian martyrs, their graves and their relics; and this the Roman authorities took pains to guard against.

Christians and classical culture

The recording of such gruesome detail is a feature of many martyr texts and even of church histories which cover the various periods of persecution under Roman authority. Accounts of dire tortures and of grim methods of execution have a dual purpose for their authors: they emphasise the saintliness of the victims, vindicating their immediate and automatic assumption into heaven; and they aim to spur readers on to greater efforts in their own spiritual lives. At the same time they fulfil a simpler purpose – to entertain their audience. In this way Christian texts act in much the same way as more traditional Roman texts, despite Christian authors professing a marked difference in approach and in priorities. The authors of martyr texts are adamant that the events they recount show the corruption and base evil of Roman society. Indeed the Devil is often invoked as an extra character – speaking either through the magistrates who try Christians or through the communal voice of the mob who enjoy witnessing their executions. Yet these same authors often follow the established stylistic patterns of Roman society in their own writings. The martyr texts are not very different in style or tone from much popular Roman literature; all that differs is the protagonists' profession of a creed at odds with the traditional Roman set of beliefs. Given the extent of the clash between the two creeds, we could be forgiven for expecting substantial differences in approach on the part of Christian authors; but such expectations are rarely met. There are two possible reasons for this.

In the first place, the authors of Christian texts were still products of their environment and society: they would have had the same education as their pagan counterparts; so their received notions of what constituted good literary style would have been largely traditional. This can be seen throughout the texts from even small points that indicate their authors' conventional education and the extent to which the mannerisms and patterns of 'classical' writing were inculcated in them. When Perpetua is first gored by the mad heifer in the arena, she sits up to pull her ripped tunic down over her thighs to preserve her modesty. The gesture is almost identical to that of Polyxena in Euripides' *Hecuba* (568-70) – a reference that would not have been lost on educated readers. Even the martyrs themselves are often described in ways that mark them out as well educated – and more crucially – educated in traditional classical forms. In an account of the martyrdom of one Pionius, which probably took place during the persecutions under Decius (AD 249-251), the martyr is described as quoting Homer at his persecutors to rebuke them for laughing at Christians who had decided to offer the imperially commanded sacrifice rather than face trial and execution. In this way Pionius not only demonstrates his own education and civilised standing within society but he appeals to the magistrates in a shared language – that of their common literary and cultural heritage:

You men who boast of the beauty of Smyrna, and you who
... glory (as you claim) in Homer ... listen while I make my
brief discourse. ... Men of Greece, it behoved you to listen
to your teacher Homer, who counsels that it is not a holy
thing to gloat over those who are to die.

(Martyrdom of Pionius ch. 4)

The classical heritage was, therefore, as much part and parcel
of the mindset of the authors of martyr texts – and of the martyrs
themselves – as it was of any well-born Roman citizen. To look
for a radical departure from its conventions would be to seek
a complete separation of the Christians from their educational
heritage, matching their division from the religious life of their
communities. We have no evidence to suggest that such a split
occurred, even in the times of greatest persecution.

Not all accounts of martyrdom concentrate to the same extent
on the *sufferings* of martyrs. Some deal only quite briefly with the
torments endured, describing even the saints' deaths with brevity:

And when the fire was set beneath him he cried out in a loud
voice and said: 'Lord Jesus Christ, you know that we suffer this
for your name's sake'. And with these words he gave up his spirit.

(Martyrdoms of Carpus, Papylus, and Agathonice ch. 5)

This is a fairly typical example of the less graphic martyr
texts, in which the emphasis tends to be on the theological beliefs
professed by the particular martyrs. A lot of attention is given to
the cross-examinations of Christians by the magistrates, during
which they are shown bravely resisting all efforts to divert them
from their faith, and even conducting theological arguments with
the authorities. So undaunted are they by the prospect of the
inevitable torture and execution, that they try to persuade their
persecutors of the goodness and mercy of Christ. Some of the
dialogues thus recorded have strong similarities to the arguments
of Socrates in Plato's dialogues. The Christians try to argue the
logic of their position according to their firmly held beliefs,
again showing the close connection between the martyrs and the
classical culture of which they were a product.

The christianisation of discourse

This brings us to the second – and much more subtle – reason for the similarities of style (excepting theological premises) between Christian and pagan texts. This reason has come to be referred to as 'the christianisation of discourse'. It refers to the way in which Christianity ultimately dictated the terms in which it was itself described and took over the position of power within the Roman empire.[22] To become as successful as it eventually did, Christianity had somehow to replace traditional systems of power within the empire. This meant not only that Christians should now manage sources of power in society – the judicial courts, the civil service, the imperial government – but even the language of discussion itself should have an overlying Christian bias. Christian authorities (and laity) hoped that ultimately everything said or done in the Roman empire would be influenced by Christianity rather than pagan tradition.

Obviously this was a major undertaking – one that had begun only tentatively in the days of the martyrs. But we can, I believe, see its beginnings in early martyr texts and their stylistic similarities to more conventional forms of literature. By presenting the concept of martyrdom for a monotheistic faith in forms that would have been familiar to any educated reader, these authors ensured that the shock of the new was not too great for their audience. It is almost like a pincer-attack: while the attention of the target audience is distracted by the entertainment value of lurid details – and by the familiar style of presentation – the real thrust of Christian ideals, embodied by the martyrs, could almost sneak up on them from behind, taking them by surprise. Thus audiences could find themselves inveigled into paying attention to Christian values almost by stealth – all the more so as many of the values of courage, loyalty and integrity were equally prized in pre-Christian society. Christian authorities then hoped the process would continue until 'christian' thinking became as natural to the audiences as 'pagan' thinking had once been (see further ch. 6).

Chapter 4

The Survival of the Church

From the first to the early fourth centuries, Christians were sporadically persecuted, sometimes on a local basis, sometimes as a
result of imperial policy. On hearing that emperors issued edicts
to forbid the practice of Christianity, that churches were closed
and sometimes even destroyed, that Christians themselves were
tried and executed (sometimes *en masse*), one could easily be
led to the impression that the religion was under constant siege
from its inception until the conversion of Constantine. And that
impression is enhanced by accounts of gruesome tortures endured
by martyrs and by the reported glee of the mobs who flocked to
their executions. It has to be remembered, however, that we hear
about this period of Christianity only from supporters of the faith,
eager to present their persecutors as agents of the Devil, their
martyrs as the epitomes of virtue and sanctity.

It is worth recalling that, if the situation had really been as
bleak as it is sometimes painted by Christian authors, the religion
would have been unlikely to survive, let alone grow to the global
position it holds today. Credit for the survival of the Church may
in fact be due to those more ordinary members of the faithful
who had been less eager to embrace torture and death for the sake
of their faith. Though they were despised by some of the saintly
martyrs, those who kept quiet about their allegiance – even to
the extent of performing traditional Roman sacrifices – ensured
that there was a large enough population of Christians, despite
terrible persecutions, for the Church to rebuild itself. In some
quarters such people were excommunicated and even regarded
as heretics; but in most cases they were readmitted to the Church
after a period of penance. This was a practical decision on the
part of the Christian authorities; for even *they* saw the need for a

strong population of faithful if the Church was to survive. Those priests and bishops who took a less compromising stance often split from the main body of the Church, establishing their own communities run according to stricter standards. Over time these split churches found themselves increasingly isolated from the main institution, even coming, in some cases, to be regarded as heretical factions themselves. This is somewhat ironic, given the fact that they had initially believed that those who lapsed from the true course of Christianity in the interests of self-preservation were the real heretics. Thus it appears that the most long-lasting effect of persecution was not the death of numerous devout Christians but rather the seeds of division sown during the period – divisions which resulted in a Church which was never fully united, even as it consolidated its position within the empire.

Eventually the severity of the persecutions waned. In AD 306 Constantine was elected as successor to his father Constantius. Under his leadership, persecutions in the western empire died out. Whether Constantine's leniency in this regard was a result of Christian influences upon him is hard to tell. There has been speculation that there was some Christian element within his household, though he himself worshipped the 'unconquered Sun'. The fact that an emperor could publicly follow his own religious inclinations in this way goes to show that it was perfectly permissible for a Roman citizen to worship gods other than those of the traditional pantheon, so long as due allegiance and attention were also paid to the rituals that ensured the continued prosperity of empire. It was after all Christians' refusal to do that, rather than the mere fact that their god was different, which led to their isolated position within society.

The 'conversion' of Constantine

The story of Constantine's 'conversion' has often been told. Following his accession to the throne, he embarked on a series of campaigns against various opponents throughout the empire, some of whom were also claiming the imperial purple. Having a loyal army behind him and being an accomplished general,

Constantine steadily defeated each opponent until Maxentius was the only remaining threat in the west. In AD 312 Constantine was preparing to fight a crucial battle against Maxentius, to win control of Rome and (by extension) the west. We are told that on the eve of battle Constantine had a dream or a vision, which promised him victory if his men marched under a banner bearing the symbol of a cross. Constantine did as the vision instructed; he was victorious on the day and the legend of his conversion was born (Socrates Scholasticus, *Ecclesiastical History* 1.2).[23] In this story the cross is taken to be the symbol of Christ and Constantine's willingness to fight under it to be his profession of allegiance to the Christian faith. But the symbol of a cross was also sometimes associated with the 'unconquered Sun' god; and some accounts indicate that the fabled banner also bore an image of the sun. It may have been that Constantine felt himself to be marching under the auspices of the Sun-god rather than Christ; maybe even more likely that he had no strong feelings one way or the other and simply used the symbol as a rallying point for his troops. The Christians were quick to claim his victory for their God; and the process by which the cross became indelibly linked with Christianity was taken a step further.

Whatever the strength of his feelings towards Christianity, however, Constantine had a tolerant attitude to followers of all religions. So incidences of persecution against the Church came to an end. In this new atmosphere of tolerance, many Christians began to emerge as shrewd administrators; Constantine was quick to make use of their talents. At some point the emperor did indeed give his allegiance to the Christian God, though he remained hazy about some of the religion's fundamental theological beliefs even up to the time of his own death. Under his auspices, however, there began a period which was almost an exact reversal of the previous persecutions. Christians were now given some of the highest ranking posts, their priests and bishops were exempted from civic duties, churches were rebuilt and, in general, new opportunities for advancement and prosperity were opened up to Christians across the empire (Eusebius, *Ecclesiastical History* 10).

The process by which Christianity consolidated itself within the empire merits a study in its own right. It was by no means accomplished over-night and traditional Roman systems endured for decades to come. However, a new tolerance extended to the Church; and the fact that it was sanctioned by the highest authority in the empire meant that occasions of persecution and martyrdom were no longer frequent or widespread.

The role of the martyr

This is not to deny that the martyrs had played a major role in the life of the Church. They had provided a rallying point for the Christian flock as a whole. Christians who felt discouraged and oppressed by Roman censorship could focus attention on those paragons of virtue and gain vicarious courage as a result. It created a sense of confidence in the Church, even in the depths of its difficulties; for a mood of defiance grew up around the martyrs and their companions, whose heroism could be appreciated and enjoyed even by those less eager to have the authorities take notice of their religious beliefs. In many ways these martyrs were the celebrities of their community; as such, their words and deeds became an important aspect of Christian culture. Just as the celebrities to whom we pay attention to today say a lot about the priorities of our society, so too – but in an even more self-conscious way – did the early Christian martyrs. We are fascinated by members of our society who embody success, be it in sport, entertainment, finance or politics. The media detail the lifestyles and habits of these individuals; new successes – or failures – are documented in a variety of ways and writ large for us to focus on. We can measure our own place in society against these larger-than-life individuals; we can see what behaviour or what possessions we could be aspiring to, or even what behaviour to avoid, as dictated by the mood of society and by those who record the details. The early Christian martyrs provided a similar focus for their society; the recording of their deeds and their successes in martyr texts acted as blueprints for the Christian style of living and as yardsticks to which other members of the faith could measure up.

There were also spiritual reasons for the importance of the

Christian martyrs. By proving themselves willing to die for their faith, they re-enacted the original sacrifice of Jesus and in that way functioned as continuing symbols of the religion's tenets. Christ's law of love – even including the laying down of one's life for one's friends – was quite literally realised in the acts of the martyrs. They carried out a similar process of salvation. Just as Jesus made possible the redemption of all humankind through his death, so martyrs, Christians believed, could help others on the road to salvation. They took their place in heaven and there interceded on behalf of more earth-bound Christians, assisting them, simply through their own shining example, in growing closer to Christ. These martyrs became the Christian equivalent to the traditional figure of the Roman patron. The typical patron in Roman society was an individual wielding political, social or financial power within the community. He was someone who could influence or manipulate situations to reflect his own interests, or those of his clients. Each patron had several clients, individuals in the community who were less powerful or less well off, but who sought to advance their cause through the intercession of a patron. The *atrium* of a Roman patron's house would often be filled with those who had come to ask favours in order to better their own condition in some way. They hoped that the patron would be willing to work on their behalf, perhaps by advancing their careers, making introductions for them or assisting them in financial matters. In return, clients 'advertised' the power and influence of their patrons, thus further enhancing their place in society.

Rather than people seeking political or financial favours from a patron who ranked higher than them in society, Christians hoped for spiritual grace to be conferred on them by martyrs who evidently possessed it in such abundance. A christianised hierarchy thus came into existence, not founded on wealth, heritage, social class or rank, but on levels of virtue and spirituality. We have already seen how many Christians opted for the practical, less glorious approach to persecution, by hiding or dissembling about their beliefs. It must have been a great comfort to those members of the faithful to know that, whatever their own imperfections, there were champions willing to fight for them and enable their redemption, even as they concentrated on more mundane aspects of life in the Roman empire.

The regular persecutions, as well as the mood of suspicion surrounding the Christians, must have made them feel under siege at times. Indeed they may have thought their world was crumbling around them – especially when they saw some of their brethren hounded to cruel tortures and gruesome executions. It was a mood that would have seemed to fit quite well with the teachings of Christ, who had warned his followers that they would not know the day nor the hour of the second coming. He wanted all who followed him to maintain themselves in a constant state of readiness, since this second coming – or the 'end' – was close at hand. As the early Christians saw many of their number become targets for the hostility and aggression felt by others in Roman society, as they saw others slip away from the Church rather than live under such difficult circumstances, it must have been easy to buy into this sense of apocalypse and gloom. This, in turn, must have helped many to contemplate martyrdom who would otherwise have considered the attractions of this world more carefully. If the world was due to end soon anyway, it hardly mattered if the Christian martyrs departed a little earlier than the rest of humanity; indeed it might work to their advantage if they could, by a glorious death, guarantee their own eternal salvation.

But the end was not nigh after all: persecutions began to relax; eventually even the emperor declared his own Christian allegiance. So the Christians needed to reassess their position within society and adjust their outlook accordingly. Since Christ's second coming seemed to have been indefinitely postponed, there was no longer such an eager rush to join him in paradise. More importantly, it was no longer quite as easy to do so. The opportunities for glorious statements of faith were almost entirely diminished; indeed they were actively discouraged by a Christian hierarchy who had learnt the importance of a pragmatic approach to the consolidation of their institution. Even during times of overt persecution, Church authorities reprimanded those who were seen as too eager to seek death; they were thought inappropriately disrespectful of God's gift of life. With the creation of a newly tolerant atmosphere in which the Church could thrive, it was both impossible and unhelpful to consider martyrdom as the highest form of allegiance to God. This meant that the Church was without any 'celebrity' figures around whom ordinary believers could rally. Some outstanding clergy managed by their charisma to occupy such a role but it is a feature of this period in the Church's history that many priests and bishops were more capable as administrators than as spiritual mentors. In fact the imperial authorities regularly issued laws aimed to ensure that only those with a true vocation should be elevated to the priesthood, rather than those who merely wished to escape their civic duties or even avoid prosecution under the judicial system (from which priests and bishops were exempt).[24]

Not only did the lack of martyrs mean that the Church was without charismatic figures to appeal to the public imagination and thus advance the popularity of the religion throughout society; it also meant that Christians themselves had to look elsewhere for their spiritual patrons. Those who had been martyred in the past would still intercede in heaven on their behalf but there was a real need on earth to ensure that there would also be up-to-date and active 'patrons' who might safe-guard ordinary Christians on their road to redemption.

It is at this point that we see the rise of a new phenomenon within the Christian community – that of asceticism. Asceticism has regularly been described as the 'new martyrdom' for a Church which was no longer struggling simply to survive but now had recognition and status within society. Indeed the ascetics shared many qualities with their martyred predecessors: their almost fanatical devotion to God; and their struggle to perfect the profession of that devotion which led to extremes of behaviour. Ascetics had existed earlier within the Church even during the persecutions. They had also existed in pre-Christian traditions. Many philosophical schools in Graeco-Roman society had elements of ascetic thinking in their practices. Pythagoras, for example, believed that an element of the divine was imprisoned in the human body, but could be given expression through silent contemplation and fasting. The Cynics advocated a simple lifestyle, detached from worldly distractions and complications. The Stoics held that passions were barriers to true philosophic living and worked to control and limit the extent to which the human being gave in to them. At the time of Christ, a group of Gnostic Jews known as the Essenes were living near the Dead Sea, employing strict discipline and self-denial in their dealings with the world. The Gnostics themselves were a group of spiritual 'pessimists' found in various parts of the Graeco-Roman world. They believed that the human body was inherently corrupt and limited. By denying its demands they hoped to enable the spirit to triumph above it. There are Gnostic trends in many of the Christian expressions of asceticism, although it is interesting to note that the Church denounced the school as heretical. The progression from Christian martyrdom to asceticism was, therefore, not an automatic preserve of the religion or even strictly chronological in terms of its development. Changed circumstances, however, meant that holy men and women living ascetic lives according to the Christian tradition now began to take their share of the lime-light, once the necessity for and the impact of martyrdom receded.

Chapter 5

The Rise of the Holy Person in Late Antiquity

The nature of asceticism

Ascetics were holy men and women who believed they would achieve maximum closeness to God by divorcing themselves as completely as possible from the world. This did not simply mean isolating themselves from the world's distractions, though that was an important aspect of their behaviour. Ascetics also believed that their own bodies constituted a major distraction from spiritual matters; so they worked to tame their bodies, even to disregard their physical needs almost entirely. According to these Christians the body's demands meant the spirit was always going to be earth-bound; this the ascetics hoped to reverse.[25] They could in that way reach the total embodiment of Christian values and virtues, thereby reserving for themselves a place in paradise. Just as martyrs had once been regarded as the recipients of a 'hundred-fold' reward in heaven, so ascetics began to hold a similar rank in the hierarchy of the 'saved', humbler mortals following behind. Martyrs had welcomed the impending demise of their physical selves, because they knew they would immediately join Christ in heaven and so become as close to him as they believed all Christians were intended to be. Ascetics, on the other hand, did not have the same immediate access to the afterlife; so they tried to bring about close spiritual communion with God while remaining on earth. Their effect on the Christian community was similar to that of martyrs, since they began to hold celebrity status in their own local areas and were even approached as the new patrons of the ordinary people, able to intercede with God because of their superior virtues. And just as the status of martyrs had increased in proportion to the cruelty of the tortures they endured, so too perceptions of ascetic sanctity increased in proportion to the rigour of the regime the holy people observed.

Asceticism describes strict denial of the body's physical demands. It is manifested in behaviour which not only ignores those demands but even actively punishes them through opposing actions. Thus Christian holy men and women regularly denied themselves food and drink, since the body's needs for physical sustenance were a distraction from the soul's need for spiritual food. Ascetics believed one could not feel truly close to God while one's stomach was wondering where the next meal was coming from – or what it would be. In any case, they should be able to trust God to provide for them; they were, after all, one of his own creations. Some ascetics also deprived themselves of sleep; for it too seemed a weakness that should not be indulged by those truly committed to understanding God's word. Others went still further, demonstrating their disgust for the body by actively causing it pain and discomfort. They would live in cramped conditions, so that the body could not comfortably sit or lie down; they would remain only standing or crookedly stooped. Others flagellated themselves, wore hair shirts or weighed themselves down with heavy chains, deliberately mortifying the flesh and offering their sufferings to Christ as a sign of their devotion.

The most famous aspect of asceticism was the denial of sexual urges – the rigorous enforcement of celibacy. For these Christians sex marked the very basest urge of physical existence; and so began the philosophy of disgust for the body's sexuality, of which strong echoes persist in modern society, most obviously in the Catholic tradition. Roman Catholicism consistently tries to legislate against homosexuality, masturbation and extra-marital sexual activity as somehow offensive in comparison to heterosexual married love. The Vatican still prefers to think of marital sex as intended for the purposes of procreation. All other sexuality is, in their eyes, although technically sinless, somehow superfluous. It is only as recently as the 1950s that Irish Catholic mothers were no longer required to be 'churched' after the birth of a child. Previously they had been obliged to present themselves before their priest in church at a prescribed interval after the birth in order to be cleansed and re-admitted to church services. Quite how revulsion from the body became so focused on sexuality in particular is not entirely clear: it seems to derive, at least in part, from the belief that sexual urges are involuntary, that a truly 'civilised' person should be able to exert control over them. This view even finds its way into Roman medical texts, in which admonitions to abstain from sex for a time are found as part of a rubric for good health.[26] he Romans felt that the exertion and excitement involved in sexual activity was dangerous – especially if it were engaged in an undisciplined manner or too frequently. Christian asceticism took this attitude one step further in the belief that lust or any thoughts of sex demonstrated a lack of self-control that could directly impede their efforts to draw near to Christ. Sexual continence was seen as the most suitable state for 'channelling' the divine voice of God – which was what ascetics were hoping to achieve.

There were also efforts to extol this position on theological grounds, as some of the Church fathers in the fourth and fifth centuries began to argue that the original sin of Adam and Eve was embodied by lust, that it was through lust that humankind lost its place in Paradise.[27] The state of pre-lapserian humans was closer to that of the angels, completely without sexual urges or needs. Procreation would occur divinely; in fact none of the Church fathers presumed to offer an explanation for this manner of reproduction – it just happened that way. The Jewish interpretation of the Old Testament concentrated simply on the disobedience of Adam and Eve, on their presumption in attempting to out-smart God. Christian thinkers, however, began to conceive of sexuality as the means by which humans expressed their fall from grace or their turning away from God. Sexual desire came to be seen as an 'animal' instinct, at odds with the way in which human nature is supposed to reflect God's own image (Gregory of Nyssa, *On the Making of Man* 16-17). The Fall, therefore, is mankind giving in to baser, animal instincts; it is to be decried on this account. By sinking to the level of non-reasoning beasts, Adam and Eve forfeited their right to remain in Paradise and were expelled to carry on the human race in pain and through hard labour. Sexuality thereby becomes both the means by which humans expressed their inferiority to the angels and the reason they were punished for it; doomed to live out their days enslaved to lust and baser passions unless they could triumph over their sinful nature. The natural conclusion of this stance was that Paradise could be regained only if lust was banished; hence the celibacy of the ascetics. There was also within the Christian community a sense of hierarchy that had already been evident in the time of the martyrs. In those days the most christian Christians were those who died for their faith. When death was no longer an option, the most christian were those who were celibate for their faith. St. Paul was one of the first to tackle this issue, suggesting that those who were able should remain celibate. Quite realistically he recognised that not many would be able to follow this course and he was quick to point out that chaste marriage was also a laudable option (*1 Corinthians* 7.8.25). Over time, however, Paul's words became re-packaged and the Church fathers' interpretation of them led to a widespread belief that Paul himself had said celibacy was a superior state to marriage. From this starting point it became easy to replace martyrs as the contemporary epitome of Christianity with those who didn't have sex and, perhaps most importantly, didn't even think about having sex. They could be described as 'eunuchs for the sake of the kingdom of heaven' (*Matthew* 19.12).

Human nature being what it is, such 'purity' was not always possible. And some of the most intriguing descriptions of asceticism from this period of the Roman empire derive from the struggles endured by holy men and women to make their bodies submit. Some fought hard against the demons of sexual lust, wrestling constantly with their bodies' natural urges, seeing their place in heaven advance or recede in proportion to their degree of success. Their extreme behaviour could only attract the attention and admiration of those unable to consider such a lifestyle; so once again Christianity was able to offer role models and figure-heads from within the body of its own faithful.

Asceticism was by no means an exclusively Christian concept. There had always been those within society who considered denial of purely physical desires and needs an admirable form of discipline; there were practitioners of this philosophy in most of the leading ancient societies. Even within the Roman empire there were those who espoused the belief that self-denial in matters of the flesh granted man a degree of control over his precarious situation in the world. One of the most renowned of pagan emperors, Julian (*r*. AD 360-363), had something of an ascetic bent, disciplining his physical self, remaining awake for long hours as he studied and espousing temperance and moderation in all things. Such a seemingly virtuous lifestyle from a man who tried to restore traditional religion to Rome and subdue Christianity, must have been galling indeed to the Church authorities.

As in the case of the martyrs, who also had predecessors from other traditions, Christian ascetics achieved a level of recognition and social status not previously realised. This was in part due to the fact that some of the best known Christian holy men and women were decidedly flamboyant in their approach to rigorous self-denial; but the real difference lies in the way their deeds and their spirituality were recorded by admiring observers, so that a cult of the holy person emerged and became a crucial part of the Church during the period.[28] It is telling that the criteria for sanctity established by ascetic individuals are often sub-consciously applied to modern Christians, so that extremes of self-discipline seem to imply automatically a greater measure of virtue than a more 'ordinary' life-style.

Desert asceticism

Christian ascetics adopted many styles and displays of self-denial. One distinct group to emerge from the fourth century was that of the 'desert fathers' – holy men (and they were mostly men) who removed themselves from their communities, taking up residence in the deserts of Egypt or Syria or in the mountains outside city or town centres, always in areas that were unpopulated and untouched by the trappings of Roman urban civilisation. St. Antony is the first saint whose extreme step of this sort is recorded in detail; his life is therefore held up as an example for Christians hoping to obtain spiritual closeness to God. He is also the first Christian to colonise the Egyptian desert for the holy man, though he cannot claim to be the first Christian ascetic. His biography was written by Athanasius, bishop of Alexandria during the mid fourth century, who, on account of his own practices of self-denial, was himself described as an ascetic even though he was immersed in civic life. He certainly admired men like Antony and his biography of the saint is almost 'romantic' in tone, painting a heroic picture of a man pursuing his relationship with God to the exclusion of all else.

Antony was born around AD 251. We are told that he had always preferred a simple life, even as a young man receiving a comparatively traditional Roman upbringing. He was not interested in the trappings of classical education, opting instead to give his attention to the teachings of Christian leaders and the bible. From this we can see that, though Antony lived the first half of his life during some of the worst persecutions of the Christian Church, there was still an opportunity to receive a Christian education in addition to the more conventional schooling. There were still regular gatherings among Christian communities for celebration of the Eucharist as well as the reading and explanation of scripture. He provides a good example both of the patchy nature of the persecutions and of the way in which many Christians found themselves able to observe their beliefs in a quiet and unobtrusive manner.

When Antony was 18 or 19, his parents died, leaving him sole guardian of his younger sister. Already his mind had turned to the ways in which he might best devote himself to Christ; he showed little interest in his estate or his new role as *paterfamilias*. Instead, prompted one day in church by a gospel reading in which Jesus told the rich man to sell all he had if he wanted to be a true follower, Antony conceived a new way of life for himself:

> He went out immediately from the church and gave the possessions of his forefathers to the villagers – it was three hundred acres, beautiful land and very productive – that these possessions should no longer be a burden upon himself and his sister. And all the rest that was moveable he sold, and having got together a large amount of money he gave it to the poor, keeping just a little, however, for his sister's sake.
>
> (Athanasius, *Life of Antony* 2)

Even before leaving for the desert, therefore, Antony had adopted a philosophy almost entirely at odds with everything that Roman society regarded as important. He had shown scant respect for the way in which property was regularly handed down through generations of the Roman family – one of the most important ways of preserving the family unit, so that property would be safe-guarded and built up for subsequent generations. That was how the Roman *paterfamilias* demonstrated his sense of responsibility and his degree of virtue. Antony simply gave away the carefully accumulated possessions of his ancestors. Not only that; he gave them away indiscriminately, not trying to keep them in the family or offer them to persons of similar social status: he gave them to the local villagers; and the proceeds from the sale of other property likewise went to the poor. Antony comes perilously close to being derelict in his personal family and financial, duties. As the family's surviving male he was legal and moral guardian of his sister, responsible for her welfare. Yet we see him dispose of the wealth and property that would have secured her place in society and ensured that she need not want for anything. Perhaps aware of how extreme, even irresponsible, this would have sounded to a contemporary audience, Athanasius adds a brief comment to the effect that Antony kept a small portion aside for his sister. She was then placed in the company of some disciplined virgins with whom to live out the rest of her days. Paradoxically, Antony's behaviour on this occasion, so radically at odds with that of the traditional Roman male, is (almost unconsciously) that of the *paterfamilias*. He has decided his sister's future without consultation; and she is duty bound to follow his instructions. He was very much within his legal rights to treat her in this way; his actions indicate how single-minded pursuit of spiritual advancement could seem almost selfish to a detached observer.

So, ridding himself quite literally of the trappings of ordinary life, Antony withdrew from society, slowly at first, then more and more rigorously. Athanasius points out that monasteries did not yet exist; also that no one had so far explored the outer reaches of the Egyptian desert. Even so Antony began a slow process of training his mind and body to serve only God, moving further and further away from society. At first he followed the example of other virtuous ascetics in the region; for his actions were not a completely new phenomenon. He prayed, fasted and kept himself busy, believing that he who did not labour was not entitled to food. In this respect Antony is often seen as the forerunner of the monastic rule, by which monks are industrious in their withdrawal from society, believing that, through their work, they are not only self-supporting but give glory to God through toil. Over time, Antony garnered quite a reputation for virtue, not just because of this obvious piety but because he did not constitute a burden on any community. Not only did he work to support himself; he also offered instruction and comfort to any of the villagers or citizens with whom he came into contact, thus slowly taking on the role of the new christianised version of community patron.

Athanasius tells us that the Devil hated to see such virtue and worked to tempt Antony, reminding him of his former wealth, of his sister and of the luxuries of life. In accounts of ascetic labours, the Devil regularly makes an appearance to distract holy men or women from their devotion to God. Some authors paint pen-pictures of actual demons tormenting and tempting ascetics. It is only human nature to have concerns for family left behind, or to recall former ease of living with nostalgia. Yet some Christians described these human longings as the work of the Devil; the body and its desires became demonised in the language surrounding asceticism. So the holy man was all the more admired: he had triumphed not just over his body but over the demons sent to make him fail. The ascetic struggle is often seen in terms of a battle in which physical longings are personified as demons, wild beasts and reptiles – one in which victory is marked by conquest of these longings. Under this scheme disgust for the human body takes an ever more prominent place in Christian thinking – a disgust which has been slow to fade away.[29] This is most tellingly displayed in the *Life of Antony*, when Athanasius describes one of the temptations resisted by the saint:

> The devil, unhappy soul, one night even took on the shape of
> a woman and imitated all her acts simply to beguile Antony.
>
>   (ch. 5)

The personification of a normal human instinct – sexual desire – as the Devil shows that Athanasius equates the two. It also indicates the strongly negative view he (and others like him) held of the female sex; woman's behaviour is seen as potentially very tempting to the ascetic; it is the work of the Devil. One of the many legacies of this period of Christian history is the view of women as flawed, sinful and inferior – a perception particularly evident in Christian discussions of the ascetic life-style.

Athanasius describes the torments endured by Antony as he worked to perfect his ascetic existence, setting them against the temptations of the life he had rejected. Antony ate once a day – not meat or wine. He slept on the bare ground and regularly kept himself awake for an entire night in prayer. Bit by bit he moved further out into the desert; for a time inhabiting one of the tombs of the deceased members of the community, which were a considerable distance from the village; then further into the dry desert; and finally up into the mountains at the desert's edge, where other ascetics came to join him and learn from him. Athanasius always describes Antony's trials as the Devil attacking him, even dealing him physical blows, so that Antony would lose consciousness or be in great pain. It is the framing of his efforts to discipline the body in terms of a struggle against a great power of evil that gives Athanasius' account a kind of mystical overtone; and this is a pattern often evident in other biographies of holy men and women. We are so used to considering the Christian religion in terms of good versus evil – of Christ versus Satan – that it is easy to lose sight of the fact that the tortures endured by Antony were those of hunger, thirst, sleep-deprivation, isolation and sexual desire. These normal desires and physical needs became terrible torments once he had decided not to give in to them. This is explained by Athanasius as the Devil's unwillingness to see Antony succeed in achieving sanctity. A spiritual explanation is also offered for the fact that Antony eventually conquered his desires; for Athanasius describes him becoming able to recognise the demons and their movements – and thus ready to withstand them. This happened only after many years in the desert; and a more rational, earth-bound explanation can be offered: after many years of fasting the body becomes inured to its effects; likewise old age may naturally dull many the keener physical desires of youth. It is perhaps natural that Antony should have stopped feeling sexual desire, stopped seeing the Devil in the form of a beautiful young woman. He would have needed less food; so occasional pangs of hunger or thirst were more easily overcome.

Antony's success made him a celebrity figure, even while he was still alive. We are told that many, inspired by his example, themselves left home and family behind, joining Antony in the desert or pursuing their own individual course of asceticism. So Antony became a leading example of a hermitic existence and is known as the 'father of monasticism', since an informal community of ascetics grew up wherever he was; and he spent time teaching them, instructing them how to overcome their own struggles against temptation. The more Antony's fame spread, the greater became his status, until Athanasius even describes him offering advice to the bishops of large urban communities or performing miracles for ordinary folk who came to plead for his intercession: he cures a wealthy young woman who suffers a terrible skin disfigurement; he saves a traveller from dying of thirst in the desert; he drives out evil spirits wherever he finds them. Thus he acted as a spiritual patron to all who chose to seek his help; they became his 'clients'. Just as the martyrs became heavenly patrons to Christians who survived them, the ascetics, too, by reason of their superior sanctity, were able to intercede with God and the saints on behalf of their clients. That sanctity was derived from their extreme levels of self-denial.

Antony's life is of interest because of its extreme asceticism and because of its inspirational effect on many of his contemporaries. Numerous Christians from rural communities strove to follow his example; even urban dwellers were impressed by his demonstrable faith, according him respect and admiration. Yet Athanasius' *Life of Antony* also gives us insight into Roman society of the day and into the Church's place within it. The saint's longevity, perhaps due to his frugal lifestyle, meant that he lived through some of the worst periods of persecution but also through the time of the Church's liberation and subsequent growth. He ministered to the victims of persecution, preaching to them and assisting them while they were imprisoned. Athanasius reports that he would have liked to be martyred himself – indicating that at this point martyrdom was still seen as the ultimate pursuit of salvation, but that he would not simply surrender himself to the authorities. On every count, therefore, Antony is portrayed as the perfect example of Christian holiness. Church authorities now disapproved of those who actively presented themselves for martyrdom, worrying that they were seeking fame and glory rather than displaying faith in Christ. Antony is exonerated from any blame of this sort and this explains how he managed to avoid execution, even as he demonstrated his Christian beliefs under the noses of the authorities. From the Christian point of view, his piety remained uncompromised. Antony in many ways embodies the transition from the time of the Church's martyrs to that of her acceptance as a state-sponsored religion. Martyrdom was not an option for Antony; he returned to the desert and continued to establish a new standard of Christian holiness – one which came to greater prominence as the persecutions eased.

Among Antony's many virtues, as discussed by Athanasius, was the orthodoxy of his Christian beliefs: he refused to be swayed or influenced by any of the heretical sects that had come into being. Athanasius specifically identifies Meletian schismatics, Arians and Manichees in the *Life*: all were branches of heresy that were anathema to the main body of the Church. Meletians became separated from the Church because of their actions during persecutions, when they took a much harder line than the orthodox Church believed necessary toward believers who complied with imperial edicts. Arians were a more substantial faction, whose point of difference was theological: they disputed the orthodoxy that God the Father and God the Son were of one substance. Manichees were followers of a religious system conceived by Mani, who tried to combine elements of different religions in order to come up with a single system that would unite East and West: they believed in a primaeval battle between the forces of light and dark; and they had an active disgust for things of the body. In this last respect they appeared little different from ascetic Christians, though they also believed in reincarnation and the transmigration of souls, which put them firmly beyond the pale as far as orthodox Christians were concerned. Antony was not drawn into any of these battles, though it is significant that Athanasius mentions them as potential threats; for it shows us a Church by no means unified or universal, even after the conversion of Constantine. Instead there were factions and sects within the body of the Church, each subscribed to by people who still considered themselves as Christians and – more importantly – as the *true* Christians. So pronounced could these divisions become, that they often spilled over into mob-violence on city streets, as ordinary people aligned themselves with one particular school of thought, upholding their position with a degree of fanaticism. Athanasius himself had to deal with several such clashes; for it was in his city, Alexandria, that opposition between Arianism and orthodoxy was particularly severe.

Antony's *Life* even offers a glimpse of the evolution within the Church of asceticism itself; for, while he himself preferred a hermitic existence, he also facilitated ascetic practices that were closer to what we understand by the monastic life today. There are those who argue, that had asceticism been strictly hermitic – or 'eremitic' as it is sometimes called – in its form, that would have led in time to its own extinction, because rigid isolation would have precluded the growth of communities of followers; so the hermit's status would have been diminished. They see the growth of a more community-based asceticism as a natural sequence, concluding that monasticism was the version of asceticism that 'triumphed' over the eremitic version.[30] Much is to do with the personalities involved. Though there were soon many more who formed their own communities – 'coenobitic' holy men – as opposed to those who lived in isolation, individual ascetics continued to attract attention and achieve fame throughout this period of Church history. It was not a case of one system winning out over any other, rather a constant 'work-in-progress', whereby ascetics worked out how best to achieve their over-riding aim of drawing closer to God. Antony sometimes had a foot in both camps, withdrawing from society but, at the same time, ready to interact with the faithful, when they came to him, and to educate others to follow his example in the future. Once again we see things worked out according to locations and circumstances – not a cohesive policy handed down from any central authority. It is tempting to fall into the assumption that, once Constantine converted, the rest of the empire immediately followed suit, that the Church took its place as the chief religious institution of empire, that there was a fully worked-out system of theology and administration. In fact nothing could be further from the truth. The *Life of Antony* shows some of the tensions experienced both by the holy man himself – *and* by his biographer – as each struggled to negotiate new paths to sanctity in a changing society.

Simeon Stylites and Syrian asceticism

Antony is just one of many ascetics who rose to positions of prominence in their regions throughout the empire; but his life is a good example of the type of struggles endured by ascetics and of the criteria for Christian virtue established as a result of their actions. Fasting and sexual renunciation may seem obvious ways to tame the body in the interests of spiritual advancement but Christian ascetics went to even further extremes. They inflicted pain and discomfort on themselves far beyond that of hunger or sexual frustration. One individual, Simeon Stylites, spent his ascetic career standing on top of a narrow column in the Syrian desert just outside Antioch; we hear of his extreme brand of self-denial from the church historian Theodoret, who knew him personally (*Religious History* 26). Simeon's cognomen, Stylites, is a direct reference to the successively higher pillars on which he stood as an expression of his ascetic life-style. He had begun his pursuit of holiness conventionally enough, joining a community of like-minded ascetics in Syria, though he quickly found their mode of existence too easy for his tastes. Simeon ate one day a week; we are told he bound cords around parts of his body to subdue the flesh. The cords were tied so tightly that in time the flesh grew over and buried them. Eventually Simeon's monastic superiors found his approach disruptive to their community; they sent him out to forge his own way. This Simeon did, retreating to a high point within the desert and living alone, communing with God. He fasted completely during the period of Lent, neither eating nor drinking. His hill-top was narrow and unsheltered but he remained there constantly. One Lent he forced himself to remain standing for the duration of his fast and, once he accomplished this, he began to repeat the exercise every Lent. From then on the periods he spent in the standing position increased, until it was almost a permanent state. As in the case of Antony, the extreme signal of his devotion to God and his disdain for the body's normal demands led to an increase in his fame and standing within his society.

People began to journey from surrounding towns and villages to ask for his prayers, for him to work miracles – or simply to gape at him. Other ascetics were prompted to try and join him but Simeon was not interested in creating another community. To escape the clamour of his visitors, he erected a pillar on top of his hill, retiring to a narrow platform above them. At first the pillar was about nine feet high and may have had some kind of stake upon it to which Simeon could tie himself in order to maintain his standing position. As the years went by, he no longer needed this prop and dispensed with it, even erecting higher and higher pillars to counter the increased curiosity of Christians who came from far and wide to hear his words of wisdom. It seems that Simeon's final pillar may have been some fifty feet in height. His 'vertical' life lasted thirty-six years (Evagrius, *Ecclesiastical History* 1.3).[31] The distance he created between himself and the rest of the world did not lessen the level of interest in him or the admiration people had for his remarkable feats of endurance. They only increased the fascination. A constant stream of pilgrims sought his advice or his intercession with God; or they simply came to witness his demonstration of devotion. Even the imperial family were captivated by Simeon's lifestyle and the emperor Theodosius II (*r.* AD 408-450) and the empress Eudocia sent to him for advice, even trying to encourage him to take better care of himself when he grew ill. Simeon wrote a letter to the emperor Leo (*r.* AD 457-474) in favour of the findings of the Council of Chalcedon (AD 451) with regard to the nature of Christ; and the emperor respectfully took account of the holy man's views.

A ladder could be erected against his column allowing limited amounts of food to be passed to him when he was not fasting. Followers could climb it to ask questions of him. He would also make use of the ladder in order to pass down letters and words of wisdom to be conveyed to emperors, bishops and clergy from far beyond his geographical sphere of influence. Eventually Simeon died in AD 459, not before a kind of cult had grown up around his particular brand of asceticism; a number of 'stylites' were to be found in different corners of the Syrian desert. Such was his impact on the consciousness of Christians that a dispute arose over the proper resting-place for his relics, Antioch and Constantinople both claiming precedence. In the end they were laid to rest near Antioch, to serve as a kind of protection for the city; an elaborate church was built around them. This is an example of the importance accorded to the physical remains of some ascetics: their relics were often deemed to have miraculous powers in their own right, since they were imbued with something of the saint who had once been physically present. It is also an example of the way in which local communities adopted ascetics as their patrons and champions, becoming jealous of outside interference, lest they lose their important 'link' to God.

One of Simeon's immediate followers, Daniel, lived on top of his own column for thirty-three years, near to the city of Constantinople. He, too, dispensed advice to the emperors of his time, Leo and Zeno. Much later, in AD 596, another Simeon Stylites emerged, also in Antioch, and, when he died, local villages literally squabbled over his body and his relics, going so far as to try to steal them from each other in the middle of the night. Not all the stylites were as rigorous as Simeon the elder: some had small huts for themselves on top of their columns to protect them from the elements; some did not stand all the time, seeing their cramped living conditions as sufficient penance. Those who achieved the greatest fame, however, were always those who endured the severest tests, managing without shelter, without sitting down, sometimes even without medical care for the terrible illnesses they contracted.

It would be easy simply to discount these ascetics as no more than fanatics. Indeed the kinds of asceticism practised in Syria are marked by more extreme forms of devotion and self-mortification than those found in more 'civilised' areas of the Roman empire. Yet the concept of testing the physical body to see what it can withstand has not entirely faded from today's world; we need only witness the stunts of David Blaine. His London endeavour involved forty-four days without food in full view of a curious and sometimes hostile public; in New York he spent time standing on top of a ninety-metre column. His motivations are considerably different from those of ancient ascetics but his experiences allow us to glimpse the realities of what was felt and endured by the holy men of the Syrian desert, as well as the curiosity they engendered. Since David Blaine could hardly walk after his forty-four day fast and required immediate hospitalisation, we must assume that desert ascetics were similarly weakened after lengthy spells without food. Blaine's time on top of a pillar demonstrates the physical difficulty of remaining standing at such height, exposed to the elements. The fact that ascetics are described in our sources as enduring their sufferings with more ease and success is probably due more to the exaggerated admiration of their biographers than to any reflection of reality. As in the case of Antony, physical hardship is overlaid with a spiritual or mystical frame of reference, through which it is easy to lose sight of the realities of so harsh a way of life. Both Blaine's stunts are excellent illustrations of the draw that such physical exertions exercise on the public imagination. The crowds that gathered to watch him were far greater than those that would have journeyed into the desert to visit stylitic ascetics; but they were motivated by the same emotions – curiosity and morbid fascination among the foremost. Just as audiences had a horrible fascination with Christian martyrs and the gruesomely brutal tortures they endured, so too people felt a strange attraction to the physical feats of the ascetics.

There were other ascetics in the ancient world who did not need to live on top of pillars to gain public attention. Indeed, if we were to believe all the accounts of asceticism from the fourth and fifth centuries AD, we would be left with the impression that the deserts had become nearly as populated as the cities. Some ascetics continued to pursue their lives of virtue alone, living in small cells or rocky outcrops in the mountains; this style of holy living seems to have seized public imagination to a greater extent; we hear more about the exigencies of their existence at this time in antique history. Other ascetics, however, created small communities around themselves and a hierarchy of authority emerged that foreshadows the monastic *Rule of St. Benedict*, in which a system of group ascetic living was established for future generations to follow. The *Rule of St. Benedict* is thought to have been published in its completed form in Italy in AD 530, although aspects of it had been known to monks and holy men earlier than this. It was a thorough blueprint for monastic living, detailing every aspect of monks' lives down to what they should wear and what they should eat each day. Most crucial, however, was the recommendation that monks should make themselves useful to their surrounding communities by doing good works (*Rule* ch. 4), such as helping in the burial of the dead, tending to the sick or alleviating the hardship of poverty. In this way the monastery could avoid being a burden on its community. Even within the monastery walls there were strict rules concerning the need for monks to work, not only to support their establishment but to avoid falling into the sin of idleness:

> Idleness is the enemy of the soul; and therefore the brethren ought to be employed in manual labor at certain times, at others, in devout reading.   (ch.48)

There were, however, still other styles of ascetic living identified and criticised in St. Benedict's *Rule* (ch. 1). Some ascetics lived a more nomadic existence, moving from place to place and depending on the kindness of the locals to support them on their wanderings. Always people were inspired by their displays of holiness and sought to enlist help within their own lives, whether to strengthen their faith, to cure some illness or to bring success in some aspect of their own endeavours. But church authorities were suspicious of these wandering monks (see ch. 8 below), worrying that it was too easy for ascetics to make up their standards of sanctity as they went along, therefore perhaps falling into immorality rather than working towards spiritual redemption. Some of these ascetics adopted the role of Christian patron with more willingness than others, interacting with their 'fans' and dispensing advice and pious wisdom. The more reluctant spent time trying to avoid company, withdrawing further and further into the desert. Others sent visitors away, contemptuous of what they saw as a more superficial and shallow faith.

It has to be noted in particular that women who journeyed into the desert to visit ascetics often received short shrift. One woman was told by a holy man called Arsenius – once tutor to the sons of Theodosius I, Arcadius and Honorius (*r.* AD 383-94), who had fled society in an effort to win spiritual salvation – that he prayed he would, as soon as possible, forget her and the distraction she posed. This same Arsenius roundly told Theophilus, the bishop of Alexandria, who visited him in the hope of some wisdom, that in future, were he told Arsenius was in a particular place, then that was the place he must not go![32]

In many of the ascetic accounts it is the female sex that is still regarded as one of the ultimate temptations facing the holy man. Women in the desert constituted a huge distraction to the practice of virtue. We hear admiring stories of holy men who never even looked at a woman and, when women came to visit them, turned their heads away, refusing to look them in the eyes. Ascetics who deigned to speak to females often rebuked them for their inferiority to men in matters of virtue, reminding them of the sinful nature that they saw as endemic to the female sex. This ability to be unmoved by the presence of women – many of them often in considerable distress – is seen as a testament to the holiness of the ascetic men in question. It was another physical temptation that they had managed to overcome. The blame for male physical attraction was always laid entirely at the door of the women. They were directly responsible for the lustful thoughts experienced by the men; they were, therefore, equated with the Devil and his efforts to turn ascetics from the path of devotion. The presentation of the female as temptress represents a school of thought that runs throughout early Christianity (for further discussion, see ch. 7 below). It has bothered many historians since; but the ascetics (and those who recorded their deeds) were following what they saw as a divinely ordained pattern. Eve was the woman responsible for the fall of man: the original sin was sex; so all women were regarded as temptresses with the potential for huge calamity if their advice was followed; little blame was accorded to Adam for following Eve's recommendations. Equally holy men in the desert did not believe that they would be in the wrong if they were to be distracted by the rich and beautiful women who visited them; rather they would be seen to have been unfairly seduced by the Devil acting through feminine wiles. Hence their often sharp dismissals of such women.

Chapter 6

Ascetics and Church Ministry

By the late fourth century it was often taken for granted by Christians that ascetics were those closest to God – the most perfect examples of Christian living within society. Just like the martyrs, ascetics were thought to gain a hundred-fold reward in heaven, leaving more conventional Christians to receive only sixty- or even thirty-fold rewards. Asceticism was advocated particularly as a way for women to redeem their sinful natures; they had more to correct in the first place and therefore needed to be more extreme in their struggle for salvation (see further ch. 7 below). Asceticism even became a state privileged over membership of the clergy and an interesting phenomenon arose at this time: many who were to be ordained as priests protested, wishing instead to live ascetic lives on their own terms rather than ministering to a community.[33] It was as if being a priest or even a bishop was somehow inferior to being an ascetic; priests were of necessity tied to the community and its worldly concerns; the ideal person of God was supposed to be immune and separate from these 'trivial' anxieties. Some of those destined for ordination felt that their new role would mean forfeiting the closeness to God of which asceticism provided a better chance. The Church, however, needed clergy to administer its growing numbers; for by the end of the fourth century Christianity had spread to most corners of the empire and, while pagan and heretical factions still existed, the Church was nevertheless able to present itself convincingly as the leading religion of the empire. Retaining and consolidating that position of leadership required extensive administration, for which priests and bishops were a necessity. This was particularly the case in large cities, where it was seen as more difficult to keep the faithful on the straight and narrow in face of the many distractions available in an urban community. So the Church sought particularly strong personalities to lead their urban flocks, and these personalities were often found among the ascetics. This makes sense if we think of the strength of character that was needed for voluntary endurance of the extremes embraced by ascetics. The church authorities believed that this strength, combined with their obvious spirituality, made some of them ideal candidates for the priesthood. We begin to see the pattern of the reluctant priest in some of our texts: Martin of Tours (*ca* AD 316 – 397), in the province of Gaul, ran away and hid in a barn when he heard he was going to be ordained; he wanted a life of quiet self-denial and devotion to God. St. Augustine (*ca* AD 354 – 430) had embraced the trappings of asceticism once converted from his former wild youth and was so eager to continue in this vein that he is said to have wept right the way through his ordination ceremony, convinced of his unworthiness to adopt a more public role. St. John Chrysostom (*ca* 349 – 407), bishop of Constantinople, actually ran away into the desert when he heard he was going to be ordained, tricking one of his friends into ordination instead; he believed that he was more suited to the life of a Christian hermit than that of a Christian priest, retiring to the wilderness rather than facing the authorities. St. Jerome (*ca* 331 – 420) had very strong ascetic leanings and he too spent much time in the desert, though he was also an ordained priest. He had grumpily submitted to ordination – a good Christian was always supposed to conform to the will of his spiritual leaders – but he insisted that he never be put in charge of a parish.

What is interesting about these stories is the way asceticism is seen as the paradigm for Christian living at a time when church authorities were acknowledging that it would only be limited in its appeal. There would always be much larger numbers of the faithful who had no intention of selling all their possessions or retiring to the desert; it was they who still required spiritual guidance and administration. It must have made sense to the authorities to seek that guidance from those who were seen as the epitome of virtue because of their ascetic lifestyles. The stories also show the extent to which the Church had at this stage to co-opt clergy in an effort to keep up with the growing extent of its flock. This marked a change from the very early days of liberation under Constantine, when people had clamoured to join the ranks of the clergy in order to be exempted (one of the perks of the clergy) from municipal duties – often a considerable drain on private finances and detested on those grounds.

Now, however, as the Church established itself more firmly within society, the pressing need for able clergy became apparent; people of administrative ability, combined with apparent holiness, became much sought after. Ascetics certainly filled the criterion of holiness – and did so in very visible ways. Some were sufficiently organised to run their own monastic communities, though others were so concerned about their own individual spiritual welfare that they were particularly unsuited to working in a community or taking on the responsibility of a public ministry.

This was something St. John Chrysostom himself admits, when he tries to explain why he was unwilling to be ordained.[34] He was a man who had always been attracted to the ascetic lifestyle, only prevented from retiring to the desert at the age of twenty by his mother, a widow who did not enjoy the idea of being left alone in her old age and so pleaded with her son to stay by her. John's answer was to remain in the city of Antioch with his mother but, at the same time, to practice a kind of urban asceticism, in which he prayed, fasted and carried out spiritual devotions with a small group of like-minded companions. Chrysostom did not believe this sort of asceticism was adequate; he remained eager to practice in a more hermitic way in the desert. When he got his chance – fleeing ordination – he spent four years alone in the Syrian mountains, praying, fasting, learning scriptures by heart and standing for long periods of time, just as the stylites did. The extreme self-mortification ruined John's health more quickly than that of other ascetics. His digestive system began to collapse and his kidneys to fail; so he left his mountain refuge and returned to a somewhat more conventional urban existence, though he was to maintain the ascetic mindset for the rest of his life. John believed that the qualities important for a life of committed asceticism differed greatly from those required for a career in church ministry. He speaks of the tact, diplomacy, good breeding, good education and strong leadership qualities necessary if a priest or bishop is to guide his flock along the right path. While self-discipline, strength of character and extreme piety are also necessary, they do not suffice on their own; and these were the qualities that most ascetics possessed. Holy men were not always renowned for their social skills, their education or their intellectual abilities. Many were simple people from villages and towns rather than major cities and they were interested more in shunning society than learning how to engage with it. John Chrysostom is insistent that learning how to interact with many different segments of the community – rich and poor – was essential for a clergyman who hoped to do a good job (*On the Priesthood* 3.16-17). So a division emerged within the Church between those who considered public ministry the highest Christian calling and those who maintained that asceticism was the superior road to redemption.[35]

St. Jerome, another ordained only reluctantly because of his strong interest in asceticism, shows all the hallmarks of the ascetic mind. He was self-disciplined, suspicious of the distractions of society and he had a deep disgust for the human body. He was, at the same time, highly charismatic, gathering about him large numbers of followers in the initial years of his priesthood in Rome. Though he had no intention of ministering to a flock, Jerome was available to offer advice and instruction to a favoured few – those who were attracted by his extreme views and regarded him as their spiritual patron. Many of them were wealthy women from society's nobility; and it was this that gave Jerome a considerable degree of power. He had the ears of leading figures in the community, preaching a philosophy of self-denial and alms-giving – as well as rigorous celibacy. When some women responded to this preaching by refusing marriage or by refusing to have sexual relations with their husbands, a crucial part of the woman's duty in Roman society came under threat. Women were important for the provision of heirs, especially at the higher end of the social spectrum. If too many of them followed ascetic teachings regarding celibacy, survival of the nobility was in danger. And Jerome was one of the most ardent proponents of virginity in the early Church and particularly out-spoken on the inferiority of the female sex. He it was who articulated the division of heavenly rewards among those who remained celibate and those who did not (Jerome, *Epistle*

123.9). Those who renounced all sexual activity were guaranteed a hundred-fold reward; those who continued to marry and bear children were entitled to a lesser degree of glory. Marriage was to be praised, according to Jerome, only because it facilitated the production of more people who could commit themselves to lives of virginity. He also believed that over-indulgence in food and drink was sinful; he and his followers went still further by fasting rigorously. One woman, Blesilla, who came under his influence was so moved by his example that she began to starve herself. Her radical response led to the collapse of her health and the alteration of her appearance within a few weeks (Jerome, *Epistle* 38.2); after only a short number of months she was dead. This caused outrage among the Roman nobility, who saw only the senseless death of a woman who might have gone on to produce further heirs for their society, The Christians saw a new martyr for their faith. This situation, combined with ongoing theological disputes, made Rome an uncomfortable place for Jerome: he departed to the desert near Jerusalem and began to live his own kind of hermitic existence.

This was not Jerome's first foray into desert living. During his youth he seems to have spent two or three years in the Syrian desert, prior to his ordination, although the details of his early career are sketchy. He tells us a little about it himself with the hindsight of later years, as part of a letter written to one of the young noble-women he hoped to have consecrated to a life of virginity:

> Many years ago for the sake of the kingdom of heaven I cut myself off from home, parents, sister, relations, and what was harder, from the dainty food to which I had been used.
>
> (Jerome, *Epistle* 22.30)

During Jerome's first ascetic stint he lived in a cave in the Syrian desert, reasonably close to some of the other desert hermits already mentioned. There he prayed and fasted, eking out subsistence existence on a barren patch of soil. Jerome was another of those ascetics who believed it important for a holy man to keep busy – both to avoid temptation by the Devil and to prevent himself becoming a burden on surrounding communities. In this respect his ascetic career seems little different from many others; what sets apart his stint in the desert is the fact that he took his entire library with him![36] He had received a conventional Roman education and was very well versed in the classics. It was here that problems arose; for Jerome believed there was an irreconcilable tension between his love of classical rhetoric and philosophy on the one hand and his devotion to God on the other. Indeed he saw classical literature as incompatible with Christian living but at the same time relished its superior literary style, which he did not find replicated in any Christian texts. This was a topic that bothered a number of early Christians: many of them felt that the style, in which accounts of martyrs and saints or discussions of theology were couched, was too simple to have any artistic merit: some disliked the Christian style for this reason, considering it vulgar; others praised that very simplicity, seeing it a virtue of Christianity that it was able to make itself available even to uneducated segments of society, that its fundamental truths transcended the manner in which they were recorded.[37] Jerome embodies this tension perfectly in himself and spends many hours wrestling with his conscience as a result:

> Miserable man that I was, I would fast, only to read Cicero afterwards. I would spend many nights in vigil, I would shed bitter tears called from my inmost heart by the remembrance of my past sins; and then I would take up Plautus again. Whenever I returned to my right senses and began to read the prophets, their language seemed harsh and barbarous.
>
> (Jerome, *Epistle* 22.30)

Eventually the tension became too much for Jerome: he suffered a fever which nearly killed him; but in the course of the fever he believed he saw a vision in which he was rebuked by Jesus himself for reading the classics. He recalls how God called him a Ciceronian rather than a Christian, ordering him to be scourged, until Jerome promised never to read another pagan work; he would only read Christian texts and scriptures.

So he recovered from his fever and would have us believe that he kept his word. He did not dispose of his library, however, and everything he subsequently wrote is thoroughly imbued with classical influences and references; he was too much a product of his culture to leave classicism entirely behind. Jerome is responsible for one of the major works of scholarship from this time: he studied the Old Testament in Hebrew and set about translating it into Latin, so that it could be accessible to everyone. His version of the Bible is often referred to as the Vulgate, as a testament to the intended lay readership and it influenced many of the bible translations still in use today.

As well as struggling to find a balance between his intellectual and spiritual inclinations, Jerome also struggled in the desert against his physical self. He ate little, dressed in sack-cloth, sat or slept on bare rock. Even so he found himself constantly tempted by memories of the luxurious life he had left behind. Through prayer and remembrance of his sinful nature, he generally managed to withstand these temptations but sexual desire was another matter. Like many ascetics before him, Jerome found himself haunted by visions of attractive women, which distracted him from his spiritual labours:

> But though in my fear of hell I had condemned myself to this prison-house, where my only companions were scorpions and wild beasts, I often found myself surrounded by bands of dancing girls. My face was pale with fasting, but though my limbs were cold as ice my mind was burning with desire, and the fires of lust kept bubbling up before me even when my flesh was as good as dead.   (Jerome, *Epistle* 22.7)

Jerome's response to this distressing situation was to weep and pray for Christ's assistance, to retire into even more remote corners of the desert until he could quell his sexual appetites. Here, once again, we see an ascetic framing a normal physical desire in the language of sin – something to be rooted out at all costs. Paradoxically this was something that would only happen in time, with the on-set of old age. Hence the tendency on the part of many holy men to consider their younger selves as corrupt and sinful.

We also see how ascetics were aware of the connection between food-intake and sexual appetite: they knew that, by limiting the amount of food they ate, they would have more success in staving off physical lust. In a young man even starvation was not always enough and this seems to have been Jerome's problem, until such time as he was sufficiently emaciated – and sufficiently mature – to have it bother him less.

One of the most interesting things about Jerome's account of his early ascetic experiences is its intended reader. Jerome writes about his own time in the desert but he does so to a young girl, probably only in her early teens, to instruct her in the best way to live a Christian celibate life. He hopes that she will keep herself away from all occasions of temptation, learning to live in chaste moderation. At the same time he embarks on lurid descriptions – not only of his own experiences in repressing sexual desire but also of the debaucheries of Roman society. His intention is that she will be forewarned against them; but the incongruity of a middle aged man writing about his own sexual lusts to a virgin of fourteen or fifteen has been the subject of much comment. Many of Jerome's writings are seen as an outlet for the physical desires and sensations he repressed elsewhere in his life.[38] It makes for some sensational reading at times, in which his writings become a substitute for sex and good food; and the fact that many of his texts were addressed to female readers adds a certain intriguing piquancy.

Jerome did not spend long in the desert on this first occasion that is described in such detail in his *Epistle* 22. It seems his passionate nature made him stand out among other ascetics more than was comfortable. The desert may literally not have been big enough for him and some of the other personalities of the day to inhabit with ease. He was also irritated by the way in which locals and clergy from surrounding areas came to him for advice on doctrinal matters instead of leaving him alone to his devotions. In this he seems to have been even more anti-social and recalcitrant than many ascetics. Eventually his outspoken views meant that he compromised his own ascetic solitude and that of other holy men. So he retired ignominiously from the desert for a time and spent time in the city of Rome, writing and working to influence the noble members of this society. He never forgot his early ascetic experiences, never relinquished his belief that asceticism was the pinnacle of Christian living; and it was this that gave rise to his problems in Rome. Once he was driven, some years later, from that city by the weight of public opinion, he decided to make a journey to the Holy Land and to return to his ascetic lifestyle. He had as his companion in this endeavour a Roman noblewoman, Paula, who surprised even the misogynistic Jerome with the extent of her virtue. She was eager to make a pilgrimage through Palestine and Israel, after which she established a monastic community for women in Bethlehem. A similar community was created for ascetic men and it was there that Jerome spent most of his remaining years. He wrote an incredible amount during this time, continuing his great work of bible translation. His relative isolation did not stop him becoming involved in some of the main theological disputes of his day. As always, these disputes were complex and heated. On a number of occasions Jerome wrote treatises in defence of the virginal lifestyle and of the enshrining of Mary's perpetual virginity in the Christian canon (for example *Against Helvidius*, *ca* AD 383, and *Against Jovinian*, *ca* AD 393). Jerome was also embroiled in the long running controversy surrounding the teachings of Origen. Origen (*ca* AD 184-254) was one of the luminaries of the early Church and wrote extensively on theological matters, interpreting the bible and promoting an ascetic manner of living. By the time of Jerome, however, doubts as to his orthodoxy had arisen: Origen denied the possibility of a bodily resurrection, believing it would only be spiritual in nature; much of his teaching was imbued with a Platonic mood or style of argument; he proposed a hierarchy (rather than an equal co-existence between Father, Son and Holy Spirit) within the Holy Trinity that seems derived from this philosophical way of thinking. These issues eventually became so contentious that to follow Origen was seen as tantamount to heresy. Jerome had begun on the side of Origen but eventually changed sides and wrote extensively against his theologies. This brought him into conflict with some of the leading church figures of his own time, some of whom still strenuously supported Origen. Origen was definitively classified as a heretic in AD 553. Jerome's involvement in the controversy in the late fourth century marks the turning of the tide against the earlier Christian thinker, but it also shows us a Church still negotiating the boundaries between heresy and orthodoxy.

As a result of Jerome's high profile in such controversies he is remembered as one of the most notorious of the church fathers, both for the strength of his opinions and for the overwhelming disgust which he held for the human body, in particular the female sex – despite his paradoxically close friendships with members of that sex.

St. Augustine

Jerome was not the only Church father to have a complicated relationship with both the female sex and with his classical heritage. Augustine was born in AD 354 in Thagaste, North Africa. His upbringing was traditional in that he learnt rhetoric and philosophy at Carthage and was thus equipped with the classical references and assumptions common to most of his educated peers. Cicero, as with Jerome, was one of his most important stylistic and philosophical models. While Monica, Augustine's mother, was a devout Christian and hoped her son would follow her example, the simple and earthy tone of the scriptures offended him and his classical training, causing him to turn away from Christianity in search of a different system of living.

Augustine spent time as a follower of the Manichees, a sect who believed in the opposition of forces of light and dark in every aspect of life; this offered an explanation for his failure to subsume his youthful desires to the demands of the philosopher's lifestyle. When definitive solutions to this problem failed to emerge from Manichaeism, however, Augustine looked for his models elsewhere; he heard the preaching of Ambrose, the bishop of Milan, and began a conversion to Christianity which he saw as the 'divine philosophy'. He put aside the concubine of his younger years, first to make a good marriage, then to live a celibate and priestly life. His classical heritage, however, laid its mark on everything he subsequently wrote and taught, if only in his opposition to it. One of his works, *On Christian Doctrine*, is devoted to discussion of how the classical literary tradition should

be subordinate to the Christian heritage on account of the superior
moral message of Christianity. At the same time, however, it made
sense for Christians to use whatever tools they could to disseminate
the message of the Church; classical rhetoric was one such tool
and Augustine is insistent that anyone who presumed to lead a
flock should acquire familiarity with its devices and with classical
references in general (*On Christian Doctrine* 4.2). His *City of God*
conducts an extensive comparison between the misguided nature
of the pre-Christian Romans and the more enlightened Christian
value-system but his classical heritage informs everything that
he writes as does a philosophy of life that owed as much to Neo-
platonism as it did to Christianity.

Other church fathers had similar internal debates. John Chrysostom poured scorn on the conventions of urban and pagan living
but was himself trained in rhetoric by the famed Antiochene,
Libanius. He was fully aware of the need for oratorical skill in
reaching his wayward flock, acknowledging the importance of a
preacher mastering the basics of rhetoric, lest he leave his charges
rudderless in a storm (*On the Priesthood* 4.5). Basil of Caesarea
even went so far as to construct a guidebook for young Christians
facing similar ambivalence in regard to classical culture (*Advice
to Young Men on the Profit Derived from Pagan Literature*). He
encouraged them to read the 'classics' by all means but to turn their
eyes and thoughts away from any sense of immorality or heresy,
such as the role of the gods in Homer. In this way they could
equip themselves for daily life in the society of late antiquity,
without compromising the tenets of their Christian faith. Each of
these writers, however, fall into the same naivety as Jerome when
he claimed to put aside his Ciceronian ways, even as he breathed
the rhythms and references of Cicero and other classical authors
in everything he ever wrote. The most successful church leaders
of this time were paradoxically those who were able to harness
the trappings of a classical culture and twist them for their own
ends. In doing so, however, they rendered themselves incapable
of ever completely cutting the cord between Christian and pagan
cultures. Instead they acted out the same christianisation of
discourse we saw earlier in the martyr texts (see ch. 3 above),
replacing one set of references with another, but making use of

these very references in order to bring about the transformation.

Augustine is also remembered, however, for the way in which his thinking on human sexuality and its implications for redemption has become absorbed into Christian doctrine and is still applied today. Jerome may simply seem misogynistic and offensive but Augustine formed an actual theology of sexuality based on his own distrust for the human body which probably stemmed from his Manichean days. It was Augustine who categorically stated that the fall from Paradise was the outcome of sexual sin; why else would Adam and Eve have felt the need to cover their genitals unless their offence against God had derived from them (*Sermons* 151.8). Other Church fathers held similar views but it was Augustine's take on the situation that was accorded the status of doctrine. He also believed that original sin was transmitted to children and that they could not be saved until they had been baptised. This has led to the creation of an entire other-worldly realm for unbaptised souls – the Limbo that was a part of Catholic belief until the mid-twentieth century.

Augustine's anxieties about the link between pleasure and sin are evidenced in the way in which he dismissed his concubine, feeling that their relationship was founded on lust rather than true love – this in spite of the birth of a son to them (*Confessions* 4.2). He subsequently thought and wrote extensively on matters surrounding marriage, sexual intercourse and contraception, declaring that sexual relations even between husband and wife were sinful unless conducted with a view to procreation (*The Adulterous Relations* 2.12). Later church authorities have built on this, further consolidating the view that sex for the sake of pleasure is somehow sinful. Augustine's own distrust of his body and its physical demands, combined with theories left over from his Manichean days, has permeated the tradition of the Church, and of Catholicism in particular.

Chapter 7

The Female Road to Redemption

Jerome is an interesting figure in his own right, largely because of the curmudgeonly attitude so apparent in his writings. His career is also important, however, for the way in which female ascetics featured prominently among his acquaintances. So far, we have been speaking of male ascetics and indeed there were probably many more of them than there were ascetic women. Yet the way of life also opened up a whole new world to the traditional Roman woman and this is something for which Christianity often receives praise. In the days of persecution women had often been martyred alongside men, though this shocked the pagans who were unused to seeing women accorded similar public notice to men – even in the matter of their execution. This female prominence arose from Christian understanding of the scriptures and the pronouncement that there was 'neither Jew nor Greek, slave nor free, male nor female, but all are one in Christ Jesus' (Paul, *Galatians* 3.28). This is often used to support the claim that Christianity brought a new freedom and equality to the female sex and to other marginalised segments of the society. Certainly, during periods of persecution, women were able to be tried and executed for their faith alongside men. Apart from this, however, claims of gender equality were almost entirely spiritual in nature. Martyred women were also spoken of in tones of surprise, that the weaker sex should find the strength in their faith to countenance gruesome and humiliating deaths, indicating a fundamental lack of equality in attitudes to the sexes. For the majority of Roman females life remained very much the same. They may have changed their religious allegiances but the day to day realities of their existence were less flexible: Roman women were still expected to marry, bear children, run households and be unobtrusive in their behaviour. Most received scant education, once they had learnt enough to administer a household. Their views and opinions were rarely solicited and, in legal terms, they were the property either of their fathers or their husbands. As always, those who were very rich sometimes fared a little better: they might even be consulted about who they would marry; they were given some power in the disposal of their own property; some of them, too, were very learned women, capable of holding their own in political and philosophical conversation with men. However, regardless of wealth, all women were expected to marry at least once and to provide heirs for the perpetuation of both the family line and the empire itself, which needed a constant stream of good-blooded citizens, if it was to withstand the barbarian threats.[39]

Asceticism offered a new option for these women. Suddenly there was a way out of the constantly expected round of marriage, pregnancy and child-birth, with all the discomforts and dangers they involved. A woman could choose to devote herself to a life of celibacy, answerable to no man, only to her God. It was an attractive proposition to many and there are interesting stories of female ascetics. Nor was it a secret why some women opted for such a life; for Christian authors openly alluded to the attractions of asceticism for women in an attempt to win more converts. One bishop from the Eastern half of the empire, Gregory of Nyssa (*ca* AD 335-95), penned a lengthy treatise *On Virginity*, in which he described the trials and tribulations of a normal married woman, contrasting them with the experiences of an ascetic female. He is ostensibly speaking to a male audience but he tells them of how a conventional woman is ravaged by the very norms of her existence, how this in turn affects the happiness of the male. Even as the man admires the beauty of his wife, he must be aware that it will soon pass, faded through age, through death or simply through years of child-bearing. Even the children themselves are causes of anxiety: many will die young – infant mortality was extremely high in the Roman empire – and they will always make their parents anxious, thus hastening the ageing process:

When her time of labour comes upon the young wife the occasion is regarded not as the bringing of a child into the world, but as the approach of death; in giving birth it is expected that she will die; and, indeed, often this sad prediction is true, and before they can hold the birthday feast, before they taste any of their expected joys, they have to change their rejoicing into mourning. Still in the fever of first love, still at the height of their passionate affection, not yet having experienced life's sweetest gifts, as in the vision of a dream, they are suddenly torn away from all they possessed.

(Gregory of Nyssa, *On Virginity* 3)

If a woman does survive childbirth, she is wearied and anxious on behalf of her offspring; the levels of stress only increase with each child she has. All the while she is subject to her husband and has no freedom of her own. She is so dependent on him that his death will plunge her into new horrors as she grieves for him, while trying to negotiate her new status in society at the same time. Her children are now fatherless or, if she has no children, then she herself is all alone in the world. In short, by Gregory's account, it is quite impossible for any woman to be happy in the conventional roles of wife and mother.

Virginity is Gregory's answer to the problem – both for men and women. Having painted his picture of a woman constantly in thrall to husband and children and financially dependent throughout her life, he puts forward celibacy as the most attractive option. Men don't have to worry about wives and losing them. Women don't have to worry about obedience to men who may as easily beat them as love them. Instead the women have as their only authority God: they become brides of Christ rather than wives of men. They owe their loyalty to a heavenly husband, who will only ever treat them kindly, who will not require them to engage in the trials of childbirth and motherhood. God will only ask that they keep themselves pure for him and direct their thoughts to him rather than to worldly affairs. Gregory believes that, if everyone knew what marriage entailed before they experienced it, they would flee from the institution and flock to asceticism instead, on account of its superior attractions.[40] He, like many Church fathers, calmly ignores the logical outcome of such recommendations; if everyone were to adopt celibacy as the best means of demonstrating their devotion to God, the Christian community would be short-lived indeed. While Gregory sees no need even to address this problem, other church leaders believed that the second coming of Christ was imminent and there was, therefore, little cause for concern about producing Christians for perpetuity. John Chrysostom once made an overt reference to the subject, announcing that both heaven and earth were already fully populated; so there was no need to worry about giving birth to still more people who would only go to over-crowd heaven should they live as devout Christians (*On Virginity* 19.1).

What is perhaps most interesting about Gregory's recommendations with regard to the celibate lifestyle is that he was most probably married himself in the earlier part of his career. We know almost nothing about his wife but it seems that Gregory regretted his married state, believing that it was a barrier to his closeness with God and his complete redemption. His response is to write feelingly about the disadvantages of the married state and to laud the celibate lifestyle as lived by members of his own family, his sister, Macrina, being chief among them.

A number of women did indeed undertake to live celibate lives, to focus on spiritual rather than temporal matters. Many were motivated by thoughts of God and heaven but, it must be suggested, some at least were attracted by the thought that they now had a legitimate excuse for avoiding marriage and all it entailed. Ascetic women were not answerable to a male authority figure. They would have no husband who owned them or dictated their movements. They would have no children to wear them out – assuming they even survived the birth. They could be educated to a higher level than was normal; they could even travel more widely than ordinary Roman women. All of these opportunities were open to ascetic females – in theory at any rate. As always, however, we hear only about the exceptional few, rather than how ordinary women fared under the mantle of Christianity.[41]

St. Macrina

Gregory of Nyssa's own sister was one of these exceptional ascetic women. She devoted herself to a life of celibacy and spiritual discipline, which apparently inspired another of their brothers, Basil of Caesarea, to found his own monastic community. Gregory wrote a biography of his sister, praising her virginal lifestyle and holding her up as an example to other Christians. Macrina (*ca* AD 330-79) was the eldest child of the family and Gregory believes that her ascetic lifestyle was ordained even before her birth. While her mother was in labour, she had a vision of the as yet unborn infant being addressed by a being bathed in celestial light and called by the name of Thecla. Thecla was reputedly a disciple and companion of St. Paul, who supported the saint while herself living a disciplined life of virginity; she had rejected the man to whom she had been betrothed in favour of following Paul on some of his travels.[42] The vision, Gregory believed, was not an indication that the child should be called Thecla – and indeed she was named Macrina after a maternal ancestor – but that her life should be similar to that of the earlier Thecla. Macrina's mother got the process off to a good start by taking charge of the girl's education and ensuring that she had no interaction with classical literature and its dubious morality; she read instead and learnt passages from the scriptures, very much in the manner of Jerome's advice on the education of young Christian girls destined for virginity (*Epistle* 107). She also grew up to be very beautiful and suitors from all around the neighbourhood expressed interest in marrying her. Macrina's father selected a young man who was related to them, apparently of steady character. In spite of her christianised education, therefore, Macrina's life had thus far been very 'traditional'. She was expected to be obedient to her parents' wishes, to marry just as every other female in her society; she must even accept her father's choice of bridegroom. Unfortunately the young man died before the marriage occurred. And it was at this point that Macrina began to exert her own will: using Christian teachings as her support, she argued that, since her betrothal had already been arranged, she was in effect married to the young man; she would, therefore, remain faithful to his memory, as if he had actually been her husband.

The concept of the faithful widow was a common and popular one in Roman society: an *univira* was a woman who had only had one husband and resolved never to remarry. The status was seen as evidence of exemplary chastity and loyalty but hitherto it was only open to women once offspring had already been produced. Macrina invoked this social model, though she herself had not technically been married and certainly had no children. Here she made use of Christian philosophy to support her stance: since her deceased betrothed is in heaven with God, she will treat his death simply as an absence; it would be wrong to be unfaithful to him by selecting another suitor. Having made this declaration and committed herself to a life of celibacy, while in theory awaiting reunion with her fiancé following resurrection of body, she also decided to remain with her mother for the rest of her days. Macrina was therefore intending to spend much of her ascetic career in the family setting – a particularly female way of living out a life of holiness and renunciation. It was not generally possible for women to set out into the desert on their own, simply to live ascetically. They could not join a desert community of ascetics, since these were all male in composition; and we have already seen the deep suspicion with which women were regarded by these men. There were almost no female ascetic communities at this time and, although a few women may have practiced some of the tenets of asceticism, it was generally done in an urban location, even in the family home. So this was how Macrina lived: she assisted her mother with the many administrative duties involved in running a large estate, concentrating at the sane time on her spiritual duties. She had established a sufficiently ascetic bearing to shame her brother Basil into abandoning his worldly pursuits when he came home for a visit. So impressed was he by the fortitude of his sister, that he gave away all his property and embarked on his own path to the monastic life. Macrina was not done influencing the rest of the family. Once her sisters were well married, she persuaded her mother to:

… give up her ordinary life and all showy style of living and the services of domestics to which she had been accustomed before, and bring her point of view down to that of the masses, and to share the life of the maids, treating all her slave girls and menials as if they were sisters and belonged to the same rank as herself.   (Gregory of Nyssa, *Life of Macrina* 8)

Macrina is described as being virtuous in every respect of her life. Gregory often speaks of her 'philosophy', by which he means her asceticism and her belief in God. So accomplished was Macrina in this respect that, when one of her closest brothers died, she was able to bear the shock with comparative equanimity and to coax her mother out of her very real despair. This would have been laudable in Christian eyes, since to grieve excessively for a deceased loved one signalled doubt about God's mercy and about the belief that all would be reunited in heaven. Gregory tells of how Macrina overcame her very nature in this respect; and this is a recurring theme in his account of his sister's asceticism. Her success in denying all worldly desires and emotions he sees as a transcendence of normal female inferiority, since the commonly-held belief was that women were less capable of virtue than men. Gregory is forced to wonder whether he can rightfully call his sister a woman at all, since she seems so far beyond the customary limitations of her sex. Macrina and her mother continued their ascetic endeavours, accompanied by their female householders, thereby transforming the family home into a version of a convent. They lived this way for many years; and a male monastic community also grew up on the estate, under the leadership of another of Macrina's brothers, Peter.

Eventually Macrina became ill and was on point of death. Gregory came to visit her. Again he praises the way in which she puts her Christian duties before her own physical comfort. As a bishop, Gregory was Macrina's spiritual superior and she is quick to acknowledge this, rising to bow to him even from her deathbed. Throughout her final day, Macrina lectures Gregory and exhorts him to remain on the path of virtue, in spite of the difficulties he sometimes experiences in a public ministry.

Their discourse is peppered with classical allusions and takes the form of a philosophical discussion of the kind that would have been familiar to any reader who knew their Plato dialogues – yet another example of the process of christianising the familiar 'classical' discourse. After Macrina's death, Gregory and her attendants discover she has been carrying a fragment of the true cross around her neck; also that she had experienced a miraculous cure from God for a malignant tumour on her chest, which she would not permit a doctor to treat because of her sense of shame for her body. Thus, in her modesty and sanctity, Macrina was again a model Christian female.

The figure of the wealthy ascetic female

Gregory and Basil were themselves prominent figures in the early Christian Church and Macrina their sister was heavily involved in their lives. We have seen how she carried out her own ascetic career while still assisting them in theirs. Other church figures also attracted female followers, who generally practiced some form of asceticism. Many of them had either refused to be married or, more commonly, had been widowed and decided to live their remaining lives as chaste.

One such woman was Olympias (*ca* AD 360-408), an exceptionally wealthy noblewoman from Constantinople.[43] She was a close friend of John Chrysostom and the two seem to have had a mutual respect and affection for each other. Some of John's final letters are written to Olympias, telling her of his worries and frustrations about how he might achieve his vision of a truly Christian city in the worldly Roman empire. Olympias was a cousin of the emperor Theodosius I, though she also held wealth in her own right. She had been married for a short while but her husband died. Indeed there were suggestions that the marriage had never been consummated, such was the strength of Olympias' Christian feeling. As such a wealthy member of the nobility, however, it was not appropriate for Olympias to remain a widow; Theodosius, in particular, was eager to marry her off in order to keep her wealth safe; for Olympias was showing a disturbing tendency to give away large sums to the poor and to the clergy. Theodosius believed that, if she remarried, her wealth would be under the control of her new husband and, as long as this was someone agreeable to the emperor, then it would be safely transmitted through the generations of the family rather than dissipated on the poor. Olympias refused. Instead she established a female ascetic community in the heart of Constantinople. She functioned as abbess of the group, which consisted of her own servants and other women from Constantinopolitan society who were only too glad to have an environment where they could realise their ascetic ambitions. Olympias' fantastic wealth was largely what made this course of action possible; even women could wield power and influence, if they had enough money and social standing. As so influential a person, Olympias was bound to come in contact with the bishop of Constantinople – John Chrysostom. She had been used to interaction with his predecessor but in John she seems to have found her soul-mate. Her convent community was right next door to his episcopal palace and the two would meet almost daily; but the aspect of their relationship that raises most modern eyebrows is the fact that Olympias regularly visited the palace purely to prepare John's meals, taking his tender digestive system into account and tailoring her cooking accordingly. We have no evidence to suggest that there was anything even slightly improper between the two; but so close a relationship can only have been charged with some degree of sexual tension, particularly as both parties were sworn to lives of celibacy. Indeed John's enemies probably seized on this friendship as a way to accuse the bishop of inappropriate behaviour. At the Synod of the Oak (AD 403), where Chrysostom was called on to answer accusations of misconduct, one of the charges brought against him was that 'he receives women entirely on his own, excluding all others'. John pre-deceased Olympias, having been exiled as a result of various controversies in which he became embroiled; but Olympias worked hard to ensure that his memory was cherished among the committed Christians of Constantinople. As one of his closest followers, she refused to acknowledge his successor to the episcopacy and was on the receiving end of hostility and aggression from his enemies, even to the point of being exiled herself. These hardships she withstood as she felt befitted a Christian ascetic, giving no heed to her own personal comfort when God's work needed to be done.

Another female ascetic who attracted attention during the fourth and early fifth century was Melania the younger (*ca* AD 383 -439).[44] Melania the elder, her grandmother, was by all accounts quite an intrepid lady and her younger namesake, born and raised in Rome, seems to have inherited many of her characteristics, brooking no opposition once resolved on an ascetic lifestyle. Even the fact that she was already married did not seem to matter to her. Like Olympias, Melania was an incredibly wealthy woman; so her ascetic instincts made a great impact on the circles of society in which she and her husband moved. Melania was a member of a distinguished Roman senatorial family, the Valerii – hence her large personal fortune. This was then augmented by her marriage to Pinianus, himself a member of the nobility. Both were in possession of property and riches throughout the Roman empire, a product of the way in which the nobility considered it their duty to pass their wealth down through the generations of the family. We are told that Melania was obedient enough to her husband to try and provide him with an heir, though she may have exacted a promise from him that she could devote herself to a holy life once she had produced a son. The two children to whom Melania gave birth both died young and she miscarried in her third pregnancy. Her husband, Pinianus, began to feel there was a divine hand behind these events: maybe Melania was not meant to hold the traditional roles of wife and mother. He consented to allow her to follow her ascetic inclinations and the two agreed to live chastely for the rest of their marriage. Not content with this, however, Melania persuaded him to redistribute much of their wealth among the poor; so they began selling off huge tracts of land from their estates across the empire, freeing many of their slaves. It was probably this, rather than their voluntary celibacy, that attracted most attention from their peers; for they gave their money indiscriminately to the poor, not relatives or friends of their own social class. In some cases they used the money to build churches, hospitals and monasteries around the empire. So one of the major landholdings of this period in the empire simply became dissipated.

Melania and Pinianus then began a series of travels around

the Holy Land and Egypt, spending a few years in various spots, eventually establishing a monastery in Jerusalem, near the Mount of Olives. Melania lived in the female quarters of this monastery, along with many women who had once been her slaves, while other ascetically-minded women journeyed from all over the empire to join her. Her own discipline was such that she was able to fast regularly, living remarkably frugally for one who had once been among the richest women of the entire empire. We are told that she even wore a hair shirt under her everyday clothes and was able to bear this, though in youth she had contracted a skin irritation simply from the embroidery on her fine and soft clothes (Gerontius, *Life of Melania* 31-2). Now, however, she had received powers of endurance from God and was granted the strength to endure discomfort far worse than that caused by a piece of embroidery. Such was her piety that her example is said to have led many to convert to Christianity – even one of her previously pagan uncles, Volusian, who was an ambassador at the court of Theodosius II (*ca* AD 436). She is even said to have been able to help Christians negotiate the path between orthodox Christianity and those many heresies that still existed within the empire. Even at the end of the fourth and the beginning of the fifth century, therefore, there is ample evidence to indicate both the survival of heretical factions within the Church and also the continued existence of paganism within society as a whole. There must have been many, like Melania's uncle, who clung to their traditional beliefs and practices, using them as an anchor in what must have seemed to be an ever-changing world.

Melania died peacefully in her own monastery in 439 at Jerusalem. Her husband, who had lived in the male quarters of their religious community had pre-deceased her. Melania's story is interesting because it embodies everything about Christian asceticism that was so threatening to traditional Roman values. She valued wealth only in so far as it enabled her to further her own ascetic lifestyle and the ascetic leanings of others within the empire. Not only did she insist on celibacy for herself – contrary to the usual role of the female within society – but she succeeded in persuading her husband to follow suit. This degree of female influence over a male member of the nobility would have deeply worried the patrician class, especially when combined with the sudden and large scale disposal of property. Paradoxically, it was Melania's wealth which made these actions possible; for it conferred a certain 'untouchability' on her; because of her social status she had a liberty unequalled in the lower ranks of society; her wealth actually facilitated, rather than hindered, her asceticism.

We have already seen something of the women who played a huge part in Jerome's church career. They, too, were drawn from the nobility, having considerable wealth at their disposal. Paula (ca AD 347-404) was unofficial leader of the group. In many ways she seems to have been Jerome's equivalent of John Chrysostom's Olympias. Certainly Jerome and Paula enjoyed a similarly close relationship and she, in response to his teachings, was eager to embrace the ascetic life. She too was married and had a number of children. She could not simply forsake these duties in spite of her spiritual desires. Indeed her pagan husband, Toxotius, seems to have taken a dim view of her devout Christianity, seeing it as a threat to his role as *paterfamilias* and his standing as a leading member of Rome's senatorial class.

One of Paula's daughters, Eustochium, came into Jerome's sphere of influence very early in her life. It was decided that she would live the celibate life to which her mother aspired. This is an interesting situation: it is hard to know to what extent Eustochium's own wishes would have been taken into account; but, if she was not consulted, then she would have been no different from any other young Roman female, expected simply to obey the wishes of her parents, whether their selection of a husband or their decision to offer her life to God. Eustochium would have been raised in the knowledge of her mother's expectations, probably accepting them as normal, just as her more conventional peers would have accepted marriage. The charisma of Jerome should probably also be taken into account: Eustochium may well have fallen under its spell to the extent that she would willingly do whatever it took to make him and her mother happy – in this case commit herself to a life of asceticism.

It was to Eustochium that Jerome wrote his famous *Epistle* 22, in which he recalls his own early ascetic experiences and explains to her what is expected of a true Christian virgin. She must be disciplined in all areas of life, carefully watching what she eats and drinks, taking care never to be idle. Much more than this: a virgin must dress in a particular way, being sure never to attract the attention of others – particularly men – through her appearance; she must not go out much in public and should be careful about those with whom she interacts. Every instruction given to Eustochium in this letter is an indication of the extremely high expectations placed upon female ascetics, with a glimpse of what happens if these standards are not met. Jerome paints pictures of those whom he calls 'false virgins': they think of themselves as ascetics but are untrue to the ascetic mind-set, thus doing more damage to themselves than if they had simply remained in a more conventional role.[45] He presents them as debased women, akin to prostitutes, while *men* who fail to live appropriately Christian lives are portrayed as effeminate, as ridiculous and even, in some places, as eunuchs.

Eustochium became one of the most renowned virgins of her day. Still Paula had not given up on her own hopes of an ascetic life. Another of her daughters, Blesilla, who had been married but widowed, was persuaded by Paula and Jerome of the superiority of the celibate life. She embraced it so wholeheartedly that she died three months later, worn out from constant fasting and mourning for her previous 'sinful' life. Jerome approves Paula's fortitude in rejoicing that her daughter found salvation rather than mourning her death. He is still more impressed when, eventually freed from the bonds of matrimony, she can realise her long-held ascetic ambitions. At this point Paula still had several children who had not been subsumed into an ascetic community, one of them only a toddler. Yet she left them all behind and boarded ship for the Holy Land, intending to live out the rest of her days in prayer and self-denial. Jerome records the departure scene at the Roman port of Ostia, the children pleading with their mother to remain and she embarking on her new life with very little by way of a backward glance, firmly fixed on her future course:

> She went down to Portus accompanied by her brother, her kinsfolk and above all her own children hoping by their demonstrations of affection to overcome their loving mother

.... On the shore little Toxotius stretched out his hands in silent entreaty, while Rufina, now grown up, with silent sobs begged her mother to wait until she was married. But Paula's eyes remained dry as she turned them towards heaven, and she overcame her love for her children by her love for God. She did not consider herself as a mother anymore, so that she might instead become a handmaid of Christ.

(*Epistle* 108.6)

Jerome is filled with admiration, speaking of Paula overcoming all inferior female instincts. It is easy, on the other hand, to see why more traditionally minded Romans would have been horrified by such a situation. If many more women chose to follow Paula's example, then there was vast potential for upheaval within society.

Jerome's admiration for Paula continues as she lives out her ascetic life. She fasts, prays, educates herself to an extremely high level in the scriptures and in languages such as Hebrew. She gives alms to the poor, constantly dissipating her wealth. She even forsakes the basics of good hygiene, taking pride in the fact that she is now unkempt and dirty, as far from her former noble and polished existence as possible. She is proud of the fact that, on her death, she has not only gone through her stock of wealth by means of altruistic activity but has left her offspring deep in debt (Jerome, *Epistle* 106.15). Paula sees this as the height of her Christian achievements. Her contemporaries could only have seen it as deeply irresponsible and contrary to everything they considered right. It is hard for us at such a remove to imagine or approve of the kind of fervour that would have led a mother to so disregard the practical realities facing her offspring.

It is tempting to think of Paula, and others like her, as women simply in thrall to the charisma of Jerome and also, as members of the nobility, being able to indulge their own whims because of their fantastic wealth and social standing. To be able to put aside the emotional and financial needs of one's children in order to pursue a reputation for sanctity may seem like spoilt and callous behaviour. It is also interesting to note that none of these women actually abandoned their superior social status, in spite of giving away their wealth and living in an ascetic manner. Instead, they became abbesses of the monastic communities they founded and gained a reputation for alms-giving and care of the needy. Many women also brought their household servants and slaves with them in their reforming work, thus maintaining their role as '*materfamilias*'. While all this is undoubtedly true, to put it down to simple vanity and whimsy misses a vital point; these women had a very pure belief in the Christian message and were anxious to be saved. Everything they were taught by the church authorities underlined their own inferiority in spiritual terms, at the same time as preaching the forthcoming day of judgement. They were eager to work towards their own redemption and at this time in church history, asceticism was seen as the straightest path to salvation. The ascetic lifestyle was the godly lifestyle and it was only natural for these women to try to pursue it in whatever way they could. Wealth was also seen as a barrier to true virtue, so they tried to disperse it in the most helpful ways possible. Naturally their good works were recognised and praised and these women held influential roles in their newly christianised groupings. Similar influence was wielded by the male church leaders. We have already seen the way in which holy men and powerful members of the clergy behaved like traditional Roman patrons to their Christian clients. It was no different for the rich noble women who adopted the ascetic lifestyle. They were accorded the same recognition and admiration as any notable Roman woman had in the past. The only thing that had changed was the kind of action for which they were praised; previous Roman matrons were lauded for their constancy in times of trouble, their restrained manner of living, their exemplary behaviour as mothers of future generations of Rome. Ascetic Christian females were acknowledged for their endurance of trials and hardships, their patronage of whole communities of those striving to be saved, their embracing of strict standards of modest living. We know little of how the ordinary Christian woman fared in this society, but it is hard to imagine any woman volunteering for a life-style as harsh as the asceticism practised by Paula and Eustochium unless there was a genuine faith behind it.

Ascetic freedom for women

Paula was not the only female ascetic drawn to Jerome – nor the only one he respected. Another was Marcella, also a wealthy member of Rome's nobility. She was widowed after only seven months of marriage but refused a wealthy and notable suitor in order to live an ascetic life (Jerome, *Epistle* 127.1). She was well educated, already being fluent in Greek before she met Jerome, and she learnt Hebrew at his urging. Contrary to his normal misogyny, Jerome has admiration and respect for the highly educated Marcella and for the way in which she would constantly question him and argue with him on a variety of scriptural and theological issues (127.7). He was possibly able to bear this with equanimity because of Marcella's diplomacy. Even if she was the one who had suggested an answer to a knotty theological problem, she presented it as if the solution had come from Jerome, flattering him even as she displayed her knowledge and learning. She gathered a group of like-minded women about her at her house in Rome and together they studied scriptures, visited the shrines of the martyrs and gave alms to the poor. Marcella's devoutness was evident in her dress as she put aside the rich clothing of a Roman widow of her class and dressed instead in plain, serviceable garb:

> She rejected even a gold signet ring, since she preferred to put her money in the stomachs of the needy than store it in a purse.
>
> (*Epistle* 127.3)

All these women had in common their willingness to abandon traditional roles and expectations in favour of self-denial and poverty; yet they were also able to do things no ordinary women could ever have done: they travelled to foreign lands and, though their motive was ostensibly pilgrimage, they were in many ways the first solo female tourists; they could also give much more attention to learning, becoming in some ways the first mature female students. Women who spent too much time being educated or on studious matters were in 'normal' society in danger of neglecting their domestic responsibilities. Ascetic women absolved themselves of those responsibilities, becoming free to devote themselves to the study of scripture, of theology and even of languages, and to engage in debate on scholarly matters with men. These freedoms, combined with the absence of husband and children, have often led some feminist scholars to regard the ascetic lifestyle as liberating for women in contrast with their previous place in Roman society.[46] While these holy women did have a different landscape of opportunity opened to them by virtue of their religious lifestyles, I find it hard to accept claims of liberation given the rhetoric of subordination that was still employed in relation to the female sex. Even as Church fathers like Jerome praised the achievements of these women, they made sure to note that the females in question had somehow transcended the rest of their sex; they were not normal women, they were saints; their successes were notable because their nature was so sinful to begin with; their learning and intelligence was only appreciated when it was couched in terms that were unthreatening to their male mentors.

Throughout everything that is written about ascetic women by their Christian biographers, there runs a strand of bemused surprise that *mere* women should have been capable of such extremes of self-discipline. The female sex was regarded as weak and inferior in Roman society to begin with but, beyond that, Christians themselves believed female inferiority had been ordained by God, embodied, as it was, in Eve and the part she played in the fall from Paradise. If subsequent women were able to rise above what was perceived as innate sinfulness, that was a matter for surprise and especial comment. We see this constantly in the writings of the Church fathers, as they speak of women who transcend their nature, who become 'like men' in their ability to suppress their physical desires. And even authors related to the women in question – like Gregory writing about his sister Macrina – speak from the assumption that the women are less capable of virtue than themselves, that any female success is more worthy of comment and surprise. So, though some may feel that the ascetic lifestyle would have been liberating for the traditional Roman female, within asceticism itself there was a double standard in operation:

the women would always have been regarded as inferior until they managed to prove otherwise. The work they had to put in to achieve recognition was thus far greater than that required of male ascetics. Through living a holy life men could aspire to be angels; the highest praise an ascetic woman could garner was to be compared to a virtuous man, even as she practically denied her own nature in the process.[47] While we hear of those who attracted this kind of praise, there were many many more silent female Christians who presumably continued to live out the traditional roles of wife and mother, their religion making little practical difference to their lives other than a change in the rituals by which they observed their faith. Certainly our evidence tells us only of extremes of behaviour in this period of Christianity – from men and women alike. Only the very virtuous or the very sinful had their activities recorded and relayed to a wider audience. The majority of Christians presumably led more conventional lives; but that, in turn, means we know very few of the details of their existence.

Eve and Mary

It is worth taking a brief look at two paradigms of female nature that were regularly invoked by Christian authorities and which inform attitudes to the ascetic women we have been studying. The first of them, Eve, is straightforward enough. She was seen as responsible for introducing sin into Paradise through her naturally inferior nature. Her curiosity and impertinence in presuming to offer guidance to Adam were seen as particularly female traits; the result was the eating of the forbidden fruit and the fall. Many Church fathers liked to see this series of events as the female tempting the male and causing him to commit the sin of lust; hence the repetition of the motif of the woman as temptress and seductress, responsible for any failure on the part of the male to remain on the straight and narrow. Eve, therefore, was the reason for the spiritual and rational inferiority of women in Jewish and Christian thinking:

> For the woman taught the man once, and made him guilty
> of disobedience, and caused our ruin. Therefore, because
> she made a bad use of her power over the man, or rather her
> equality with him, God made her subject to her husband.
>
> (John Chrysostom, *Homily 9 on 1 Timothy*)

Each woman was, therefore, another Eve; morally and rationally
inferior by nature, but also dangerously liable to lead to sin on the
part of men (Tertullian, *On Women's Dress*).

At the other end of the scale we have Mary, the Virgin Mother of
God. Mary's role as the archetypal virgin allowed her to be declared
as sinless and therefore a fitting vessel for the Son of God. Her
virgin status was the subject of much debate however. During the
fourth and fifth centuries a number of discussions were held as to
whether Mary remained virgin after giving birth to Jesus. Some felt
she would have resumed married life with Joseph and even given
birth to other children. But this position became steadily down-
played, just as celibacy became more and more the ideal state for
luminaries in the Christian world. There were others who worried
that Mary could not have retained her virginity because of the very
act of giving birth to Jesus. Even this problem was resolved when
her perpetual virginity became (following the Council of Chalcedon
in AD 451) a matter of doctrine in the Christian Church – a divinely
facilitated mystery that led to celibacy becoming one of the most
prized aspects of Christian behaviour.

Mary was also a second Eve, however; one who could redeem
the failings of her 'ancestress' by embodying the opposite standard
of behaviour. Mary's virginity reversed Eve's Fall and pointed the
way to redemption:

> Death came through Eve: life has come through Mary. For this
> reason the gift of virginity has been poured most abundantly
> upon women, seeing as it was from a woman that it began..
>
> (Jerome, *Epistle* 22.21)

Mary was sinless as the Mother of God; but this purity was interpreted as a freedom from any sexual taint. This further reinforced the belief that sexuality was both equated with sinfulness and was somehow the 'original sin' of Eve. It is interesting to note that the cult of the Virgin Mary began its significant growth in the fourth and fifth centuries, just as asceticism became prized as the perfect Christian lifestyle. In the New Testament and in the writings of the early years of the Church (e.g. the apocryphal gospels, discarded from the final biblical canon) the focus was on Mary's role as mother of Christ and as obedient servant of the Lord. Her virginity and corresponding moral purity was only highlighted at a later stage and the insistence on her freedom from sexual stain was extended even to her own immaculate conception. The belief that she herself had been conceived without the sin of carnal behaviour was important for one who was herself to be a pure vessel for Christ. Mary's immaculate conception was introduced as a doctrinal certainty in the Catholic tradition in 1854 and is still a central tenet of the faith today. Suspicion regarding human sexuality and the promotion of extreme virginity as a path to redemption is therefore enshrined in modern versions of Christianity.[48]

Chapter 8

'Illegal' Forms of Asceticism

The holy men and women so far considered were exemplars of ascetic behaviour; from their achievements arose an accepted paradigm of ascetic living but the paradigm was not always followed and there arose ascetic practices that came to be frowned on by church authorities.

It was generally thought important that ascetics contribute toward their society in some way, to avoid being a burden on the ordinary community: St. Antony insisted on working to support himself, weaving baskets or tilling the soil; even Jerome had a small vegetable patch outside his cave; Melania (both elder and younger) and other female ascetics took on pastoral roles, caring for the sick and poor in their localities, sometimes even ministering to an equivalent community of male ascetics. This all kept the holy people from undesirable idleness and hard work came to be equated with a form of devotion to God. It was also important from a practical point of view, particularly when ascetic communities grew in size. If these communities did not try to be self-sufficient, relying instead on ordinary Christians in their society for support, that society could become severely stretched. So ascetics who carried out some form of manual labour in conjunction with their spiritual devotions thought of themselves as following Christ's teachings regarding the danger of idleness. A symbiotic relationship between themselves and the locals existed, so that both flourished. The ascetics offered prayers for those in the community, functioning as its spiritual patrons, interceding with God and the saints on its behalf. In large measure they also saw to their own upkeep, though the local faithful would be willing and able to make up any shortfall, often expressing their status as spiritual 'clients' by making substantial gifts to the monastic communities.

There were, however, ascetics who claimed to follow a separate line of Christ's teaching – that believers should not worry who would provide for them, since God looked after even the flowers in the field and the sparrows in the air.[49] Manual labour in any form would distract them from proper focus on their spiritual quest to grow closer to God. They could offer prayers on behalf of their local community, maintaining the patron-client relationship; but their position could be described as almost parasitic. The locals would supply them with food and shelter – a relationship that remained sustainable only where the ascetics were few in number and sparsely distributed. As entire communities of monks began to form, the strain on local resources became much greater. Some regions were unable to support their monastic members and this led to a kind of nomadic asceticism. Looking to be supported almost entirely by others, groups of monks would travel from place to place, staying so long as a community could support them, then moving on. During the later Roman empire, many communities could barely support themselves, still less large groups of travelling monks, who seemed to contribute nothing tangible to society. It was therefore a practical problem – and one that was not only a question of logistics.

Wandering monks constituted a threat to the local, more conventional church authorities; and they were frowned on for this reason. The received wisdom of the Church was that ascetics should work to support themselves. Those who did not were thus already in contravention of church rulings; at the same time ascetics and ordained clergy were often at odds over the hierarchical systems in operation in early Christianity. Ascetics saw themselves as answerable only to God – hence their isolated existence. Those who lived a coenobitic form of asceticism viewed their abbot as their authority figure but, even then, their community as a whole was generally at some remove from the rest of society. It was difficult for some of them to accept the authority wielded by priests and bishops who were so far detached from them and their lifestyle. To refuse such authority was to run the risk of being branded heretical: a number of disputes arose during this period between ascetics and members of the urban clergy. Monks who did not obviously acknowledge the authority of the priests or bishops of the Church became forces for disruption – a problem exaggerated if they travelled in packs through regions of the empire, fomenting unrest among those very communities on whom they depended for support. In AD 388 for example a band of travelling monks burned a synagogue near the Euphrates. In 391 the bishop of Alexandria, Theophilus, called on them to tear down the shrine of Serapis in the city. So far, these monks took it upon themselves (or were encouraged) to target non-Christian sects but in North Africa a group of wandering ascetics roamed around the great estates, ransacking them in an expression of their version of devotion to God. In 407, when John Chrysostom was exiled to Caesarea, the bishop of the area encouraged a group of monks to terrorise supporters of the former patriarch. The fact that St. Benedict in his *Rule* (*ca* AD 530) can identify wandering ascetics as a distinct group, denouncing them as the worst kind of monk, indicates the extent to which they threatened the authority of the Church and the harmony of the community:

> But the fourth class of monks are those called '*girovagi* (literally those going about the land)', who spend their whole life going from one province to another, staying three or four days at a time in different cells as guests. Always roving and never settled, they indulge their passions and the cravings of their appetite, and are in every way worse than the Sarabaites (ascetics who lived in groups of two or three and made up their own rules about what constituted holy behaviour). It is better to pass all these over in silence than to speak of their most wretched life. *(Rule of St. Benedict* ch. 1)

An example of this way of life can be found in the career of Alexander the Sleepless (*ca* AD 355-427), a monk who gathered a band of followers and travelled throughout Syria and Asia Minor at the end of the fourth and in the first half of the fifth century.[50] He is called Alexander the Sleepless because part of his regime was to sing hymns and offer prayers to Christ at hourly intervals throughout the entire twenty-four hours of the day. This left little time for sleep. These devotions may only have been offered at certain points in the liturgical year but they were sufficient to get him his nickname. Alexander was motivated by thoughts not unlike those of St. Antony many years before: on hearing the scriptural call, to sell everything, to give the proceeds to the poor and to follow Christ – taken as an instruction to him personally. He retired to the desert, joining a community of monks for his early ascetic endeavours. His interpretation of true asceticism proved very different from that of the other members of his community: he saw how the abbot constantly had to take care that each brother was provided for, instead of being free from such cares and able to devote his attention to God; he also saw how the monastery as a whole accumulated property and possessions in contravention of Jesus' instruction to 'take no care for tomorrow'. He challenged his fellow monks, asking why they did not follow the gospel in this respect; they replied that it would realistically be impossible to live in that way. This made Alexander angry; he felt he had wasted his ascetic years to this point in a community too lazy to bring the gospel to life on earth. He departed from them and went to the desert. His challenging of the order accepted by those ascetics with whom he was living already shows the potential for disruption within society and the Church over differing inter-pretations of the gospel.

Alexander journeyed about through the desert, praying and taking no heed for the practical concerns of daily life – yet he was always provided for. Locals offered him food and shelter, though many of the occasions when he is provided for are described in terms of miraculous interventions from God or his angels. This lends support to Alexander's approach to asceticism, proving his faith by God's ability to provide for his followers. He visited cities and converted people there – pagans to the Christian way of life and Christians to his own form of asceticism. The presence of so charismatic a monk within city walls, one who preached a doctrine opposed to that offered by the priests and bishops regularly ministering to the urban flock, was a potentially dangerous element according to church thinking. Alexander disapproved of anyone who claimed to follow Christ, yet remained concerned to gather and maintain possessions; so he was at odds with the procedures of the conventional church authorities. Nor did he keep his opposition quiet: he spoke out boldly against what he regarded as corruption within the ranks of the Church, deeply threatening its established authority. In some quarters he came to be regarded as a heretic.

Alexander's career continued in much the same vein – some periods passed in the desert (including many years when he spent his nights in a storage jar, buried in the sand), others in towns or garrison-posts around the empire, preaching his version of Christian doctrine and winning many followers. These followers often remained baffled as to how they might survive under Alexander's rule of not worrying how they would eat or drink; but there seemed always to be a supply of food, sometimes delivered under 'miraculous' circumstances. Alexander saw this as vindication of his faith in God – soldiers making their food rations available to the wandering band of monks, a baker 'spontaneously' delivering his fresh batch of loaves to their door. The baker in question claimed that a man dressed in shining white appeared before him just as he was taking the bread out of the oven, telling him to deliver it to Alexander's group (*Life* [see note 50] ch. 45). These 'miracles' of provision were more likely to have been the normal response of ordinary citizens of empire encountering for the first time such extreme examples of holiness. They voluntarily supplied food and shelter where needed, seeking the intercession of the holy man on their behalf in return. Even without the Christian frame of reference, it is unlikely in the ancient context that people would have failed to offer hospitality and assistance to a band of travellers pitching up on their doorstep; mutual support was an important aspect of survival. The concept of hospitality (*xenia*) was also enshrined in Graeco-Roman society as a code to which every civilised person would be expected to adhere.

Not everyone was always overjoyed to see these monks arriving in their locality. In one instance the citizens of Palmyra shut their gates tight against them, saying that they could not possibly feed so many men, that, if the monks were welcomed in, the ordinary inhabitants would starve (*Life* ch. 35). And this incident demonstrates the force for disruption these wandering ascetics could pose, especially in large numbers. More and more they were denounced by authorities of the core 'orthodox' tradition. Coenobitic ascetic living became the accepted norm, since it remained within the hierarchy of the Church and did not threaten the well being of the surrounding peoples.

Transvestite asceticism

The struggle to live an ascetic life was, as we have seen, always more difficult for women. Not only did they have to strive harder to overcome innate sinfulness and inferiority: they had to defy centuries of cultural conditioning, which said that they could only be wives and mothers, that they were at the disposal of the male authority figures in their families. Not every Christian woman who declared her intention to live celibately and in devotion to God was applauded by her family; some found themselves actively cut off from relatives and friends. Communities for ascetic women, like those founded by Macrina, Melania and Paula were few and far between; they tended to consist of rich women and their own households; so word of their asceticism would not necessarily have spread much beyond their immediate locality, unless they had connections with one of the prominent Church fathers such as Jerome. Even if news of them *had* spread, not every woman could have made the journey to the Holy Land or Caesarea to join them. Nor could women less rich simply establish their own ascetic households; they would have no means of supporting themselves. Equally, it was difficult for women to live the more hermitic existence preferred by ascetics who headed for the desert alone; they were held to be at greater risk of attack by brigands and outlaws – something perceived as less true of male ascetics. Many women had to find other ways of living out their ascetic ambitions.

A few, it seems, headed into the desert alone but, crucially, they adopted a disguise that went some way to ensuring their relative safety. There are a number of stories of women who adopted male dress, explaining their beardless state by claiming to be eunuchs. Sometimes they lived alone; more often they joined a community of male ascetics, living as men or as eunuchs until they died.[51] The true nature of their sex was frequently only discovered when they were laid out for burial. Eunuchs as a group were a generally despised in the later Roman empire; there was a degree of disgust at their physical state, which would have prevented close enquiries being made by their chosen companions. In addition Christian mistrust of the body would have led to an exaggerated modesty among holy men who shared a living space according to the proper standards of asceticism; so it is quite conceivable that such women could have escaped notice for long periods of time. The most famous such woman was Pelagia of Antioch who lived as a prostitute in her youth. She underwent a dramatic conversion to Christianity – we know little about the catalyst for this shift but it seems to have followed from the preaching of the bishop Nonnus who was visiting Antioch for a conference (*ca* AD 400-450). She then departed from the city and journeyed to Jerusalem to live as a eunuch hermit by way of penance for her previous life, her true sex being discovered only after her death. Little else is known about this Pelagia; attention to her life would have been focused on the extent of her debauchery before her conversion and the contrast in her behaviour after it. Other tales of transvestite ascetics follow a similar pattern – monks coming upon a female who had been living ascetically and solitarily in male guise just in time to bury her and discover the truth about her sex (*Sayings of the Fathers* 4 and 63). It is interesting to note, however, that the motif of the transvestite female was a popular one throughout Roman literature, featuring in a number of comedies prior to the final plot resolution. The cross-dressing ascetics recorded in accounts of Christian desert asceticism acknowledged the popularity of this kind of plot; it was a useful way of encouraging the faithful to focus on examples of piety and hence could even be an example of the way in which the discourse of the day was relentlessly christianised, adopting classical motifs and reworking them in Christian terms. Such ascetics seem, however, to have been more than literary devices in attempts to revamp the discourse of the day, if only because church authorities were so anxious about the phenomenon.

It was a situation that bothered church authorities when they came to hear of it. There survive a number of rulings from church councils that struggle to legislate for the practice of transvestite asceticism. The councils were deeply disapproving of women who adopted male dress or even cut their hair, declaring that any woman acting in this way to adopt an ascetic lifestyle should be excommunicated. They were particularly anxious about the scope for disruption and confusion between the sexes that could arise; and they tried to insist that gender divisions should be clearly demarcated and observed.[52] There were fears, too, that women, even in the guise of eunuchs, would distract male ascetics from their vocations – a view that once again laid responsibility for male sin at the door of the female. There were even cases where the transvestite females found themselves accused of impregnating local women who had come to them for instruction, such was the success of their disguise (e.g. *Life of Mary, Lausiac History* 2.26). The phenomenon, however, shows the extent to which gender was much more a matter of performance than appearance during this period: so long as these women acted in sufficiently male ways, they often escaped detection. And practising ascetic virtue was seen as a particularly male thing to do. Men were considered capable of such virtue to a far greater extent than women; so a successful holy person who appeared male was automatically accepted as male, since behaviour and appearance matched perfectly.

Cohabiting virgins

Another way in which holy women struggled to create an ascetic space for themselves was to live with a male ascetic, keeping a kind of monastic household within the conventional community. Cohabiting monks and virgins were a source of deep anxiety to church authorities, who saw potential for all sorts of temptation and sin in such arrangements.[53] It was a predominantly urban arrangement, where women, unable to live ascetically, like Macrina, within their own families or to afford their own establishment or to join a community such as the one founded by Paula at Bethlehem, could live in the same household as other ascetically-minded people. The male ascetics would be able to support the household financially, the women administered it domestically. Both claimed to have only spiritual matters at heart and promised to remain celibate.

It was much like the situation of the priest's housekeeper living in the priest's house which was so prevalent in twentieth-century Ireland – a stereotype invoked to great comic effect in the characters of Mrs Doyle and Father Ted in the 1990s Channel Four comedy, the eponymous priest being incapable even of making his own cup of tea on Mrs Doyle's night off. The ascetic men of late antiquity claimed that they too were incapable by reason of their gender of carrying out household duties such as cooking, laundry and sewing; the women by reason of theirs that they did not know how to manage finances or protect themselves from the outside world. Each inhabited traditional stereotypes, the only new departure being their celibacy. There were also those who suggested that, by so exposing themselves to temptation and triumphing over it, they were accumulating a greater share of the heavenly reward for themselves, having endured more hardship. Not surprisingly, some cohabiting ascetics – or *subintroductae* as they were labelled – failed to withstand temptation and there are many stories of fallen virgins betrayed by their pregnant bellies, even by the toddlers they carried around with them.[54] Church authorities were disgusted by this behaviour, working hard to combat it: they poured scorn on these women, accusing them of bringing the entire institution of celibacy into disrepute, making Christians the laughing stock of pagans and damning to eternal punishment not only themselves but the male ascetics involved. Many authors penned texts on the subject: two treatises by John Chrysostom perhaps provide the most complete picture of what was involved (*Instruction and Refutation Directed Against those Men Cohabiting with Virgins* and *On the Necessity of Guarding Virginity*). He was deeply distressed by women who acted in so forward a way as to invite male ascetics to live with them, to tease them with their bodies, though never delivering on their implied promise. They kept the men in permanent frustration and were thus responsible for every lustful thought the men might have, distracting them from God.

He also rebukes the men who have become so enfeebled as to follow without demur the bidding of women; he paints a number of skilful pen portraits of male ascetics emasculated to the point that they carry out domestic errands for the women without so much as a murmur, even proud of their servile state, parading to church as escorts of these women, instead of shunning them as the semi-prostitutes they were:

Indeed, these men will not refuse to devote themselves to matters concerning women's paraphernalia; instead they will constantly be stopping in at the sliversmith's to inquire if the mistress' mirror is ready yet, if he has finished the urn, if he has delivered the perfume flask … from there he runs again to the perfume maker to discuss aromatics for his mistress and often he will not hesitate in his abundant zeal to insult the poor fellow.

(Instruction and Refutation Directed Against those Men Cohabiting with Virgins 9-10)

The male ascetic living with a group of women is at risk of embarrassment even as he moves about his own house:

When day breaks and both must arise from bed, watch out! Be on guard! She cannot set foot into the outer room without trepidation, for often when she enters she runs the risk of rushing headlong into the naked body of the man. And he himself, anticipating this, sometimes comes in after he has announced himself beforehand, yet sometimes he enters incautiously and becomes the butt of uproarious laughter.

(On the Necessity of Guarding Virginity 11)

In this form of cohabitation John saw women behaving like men, men like women; not surprisingly, he felt the natural order of the world crumbling about his ears. Jerome also has choice words about these ascetics, openly accusing the women of actually sleeping with their male housemates – of fornication and lust (Jerome, *Epistle* 22.13-14). However, in spite of all the anxieties expressed about this practice, it seems to have become quite widespread and there are scholars who believe it spread even as far as Britain and Ireland. The practical attractions of such a way of life – particularly for poor female ascetics with more limited scope to express their ambitions – outweighed the disapproval of the more orthodox church authorities.

Conclusions

What has gone before is only the briefest of introductions to the subjects of martyrdom and asceticism within the Christian Church in late antiquity. Each area is a rich and complex one in its own right. And we are fortunate that this period of Roman history is well documented. This is largely because of the survival of Christian documents, detailing the sufferings of martyrs or the feats of endurance by holy men and women. It is something of a truism that history is written by the 'winners'. The Church may be seen as winner in the sense that it emerged as the dominant power base within the late Roman empire – and even out-lived the empire.

Many of the events recorded in these Christian texts incorporate elements of fantasy or the incredible. Seeking verification for miraculous occurrences, however, misses the point. The language of miracles and wonders was a way of making the central mysteries of the faith accessible to a universal audience, reaching Christians of all social classes and standards of education. Of course many people believed fervently that such amazing things could happen; that an angel could direct a baker to deliver his first loaves of the day to a band of wandering monks; that a young noble woman could withstand all manner of tortures and humiliations in the arena without even noticing her terrible injuries. We must always be wary of donning twenty-first century spectacles to view this period in history. Even where disbelief cannot be so willingly suspended, the retelling of superhuman feats and miracles provides a focus for a disparate audience – and a point of common reference for all believers. Nor should the sheer entertainment value of such stories be underestimated; the fascination of the lurid details could capture the imagination and hence the loyalty of lay Christians far more effectively than complex debates about theology. Each tale of an incredible but divinely prompted event should, therefore, be read on multiple levels; for it offers a key to the achievement of Christianity in successfully dominating the social and power discourses of the period.

In AD 410, during the lifetime of some of the ascetics we have discussed, Rome was invaded by 'barbarians', under the leadership of Alaric the Goth. It was a major culture-shock to all who considered themselves citizens of the empire. The very heart of their empire was suddenly under foreign control and it must have seemed as if everything they had ever taken for granted was in danger of disappearing. Jerome was deeply disturbed by what had happened to his former home, considering himself lucky to be safely removed in his monastery in Bethlehem. St. Augustine was so moved by the sack of Rome that it provided the impetus for his mammoth work *City of God*, in which he tried to explain how the Christian God could preside over a world in which such things happened, while still claiming to be merciful and loving. Yet it has to be said that the immediate shock of the invasion was probably the greatest aspect of the trauma experienced by the late Romans. Life in the city of Rome – and in the empire as a whole – did not change substantially even after the barbarian tribes had entered the city. Indeed there is much to suggest that Alaric and his troops did a great deal to emulate the Roman way of life rather than destroy or change it. Day-to-day life went on with very little difference for several decades to come. This extended to religious rituals. Christian services continued and the church fathers continued to manage their wayward flocks by preaching, by issuing doctrinal edicts and by writing numerous treatises and letters.

There remained pagans in cities and towns throughout the empire: in AD 415, a pagan philosopher was murdered by a lynch mob in the city of Alexandria. It was an event much decried by Christians and pagans alike, particularly because the philosopher in question was a noble woman, reputedly very virtuous. Hypatia had been a teacher of philosophy and mathematics at her father's school in Alexandria and it does not seem that they wanted for pupils, even at the start of the fifth century when Christianity had been the favoured religious philosophy for almost a century. Hypatia and her family were pagans, practicing traditional Roman religious rituals and turning to philosophy for moral guidance and explanations of their place in the world. Some of their pupils were also pagan but many were Christians availing themselves of a traditional education, within which philosophy would have been an intrinsic part. So the two belief systems could often co-exist, Christians willing to adopt what they needed from the pagans, even as they tried to write them out of history.

This inter-dependence of Christianity with elements of classical philosophy is a recurring theme; we saw Augustine's writings constantly overlaid with a Neo-platonist flavour (see ch 6 above). As part of the process of the christianisation of discourse, Christian writers and thinkers invoked and appropriated all the powerful models of their classical heritage as a means both of reaching their audience and of establishing their social dominance. Neo-platonism as a school of thought was absorbed into the thinking of many church fathers, since philosophy was a crucial aspect of the standard education of a well-to-do young man in the later Roman Empire. It comprised the revitalisation of the teachings of Plato, with particular reference to his theories about the nature the divine; and it provided a model for truly philosophic living. Indeed Neo-platonism had much in common with Christianity. One of the most devout proponents of the Neo-platonic lifestyle was the emperor Julian (r. AD 360-363), the last of the rulers of the empire who proclaimed his allegiance to the pagan system of religion and who even tried to reverse Christian advances in society. Ironically, Julian lived a life that could easily be described as ascetic, holding similar beliefs to the Christians about the importance of subordinating bodily desires in the search for true wisdom and virtue. The motives and the actions were similar; it was simply the labelling system that differed.

There were always tensions of the kind evidenced by the death of Hypatia herself. She was allegedly torn to shreds by a mob led by monks and by the right hand man of Alexandria's bishop at the time, Cyril. These Christians felt Hypatia's teachings – and her close contacts with the secular authorities of the day – posed a threat to their position in society. Indeed Christians, far from complacent about their success and their spread, remained wary of anything which might constitute a threat to their position of strength: pagan temples were often destroyed by angry crowds;

and there were frequent clashes between gangs of citizens upholding opposing beliefs. It was a turbulent time for pagan and Christian alike – one far from the smooth and joyful triumph of the Church that is sometimes presented. Nevertheless, the Church steadily took on the position of power within the empire: church and state became closely inter-twined, emperors regularly seeking advice from bishops, who could therefore influence the progression of secular events. There was still a sense of unease about the future, as the borders of empire began to give way before barbarian assaults and it would have been easy for Christian leaders to tap into this anxiety, presenting their faith as the sole way to comfort and protection. In fact that was very much what traditional Roman religion used to do; and now we see Christianity taking over the protective role and becoming important to people in that regard.

Eventually Rome fell in a true military sense. Invasions became more and more frequent; the western half of the empire could no longer support itself and broke apart. By the start of the sixth century it was a very different place: administrative systems had broken down; local power brokers took over; the beginnings of the feudal system – such a feature of medieval Europe – even made their appearance. This was a pre-cursor to what are sometimes called the 'dark ages', as different tribes throughout Europe tried to negotiate new paths for themselves in the absence of the dominant leadership that Rome had provided. With traditional authority systems gone, the Christian Church often became the focus of many people's attention. And during this period it was able to wield considerable power. Monastic communities, in particular, were key elements of this society, providing a sense of stability as well as a crucial feeling of comfort. As ascetics had fulfilled the role of spiritual patrons to the communities around them, so did the monks of medieval Europe. Now, however, the ascetics were grouped together, living under an established order or system, often owning or building their own structures for living, for work and for worship – buildings which became important fixtures in the landscape. Hermits continued to exist, though perhaps in smaller numbers; it was monastic asceticism that came to have the most public presence. Classical culture was almost utterly replaced by Christian doctrine and folklore. The church authorities became the new elite of the society and the possessors of the accepted standards of knowledge and education.

In the eastern empire, however, things took a somewhat different course. Far from segregating themselves from the systems of government, the Christians in the eastern empire integrated themselves into the life of the imperial court and its administration more thoroughly than ever. Modes of government remained recognisably 'Roman' for many years to come and the inhabitants of this world of Byzantium still protected their cultural links to the old Roman empire. The classical heritage was still prized by the educated members of this society, among whom church authorities continued to number. In AD 533, the emperor Justinian II invaded north Africa and western Europe in order to restore the 'lost' provinces of Rome to his territory. His action shows two things: in the first place the division between east and west had become pronounced enough for these provinces – formerly the heartland of the Roman world – to be considered lost; in the second place Justinian's campaign shows the extent to which citizens of the eastern empire still considered themselves 'Romans' with a mandate to restore lost territory in spite of the fact that their seat of government was in Constantinople and their cultural influences were being drawn ever more steadily from the orient instead of the west.

Pressures were increasingly brought to bear on the Byzantine world from Persia and the Arab world into the sixth and seventh centuries AD. The response of the eastern empire was to 'circle the wagons', consolidating its beliefs and its social structures in opposition to the oriental threat. So, a focused and elaborate version of Christianity developed inside the walls of Constantinople, echoes of which remain in the Orthodox tradition of eastern churches today. As time went on, however, the expression of this devotion turned ever inwards as the boundaries of the traditional eastern Roman empire shrank back to the walls of Constantinople itself and as Islam began its rise as the newly dominant faith in this part of the world. The two halves of the former Roman empire became irrevocably split and the locus of power and culture shifted to Byzantium and further east. The

Christian Church also fragmented and developed according to different modes and systems, but this is beyond the scope of this volume.

Martyrdom was naturally was much less of an issue as time progressed, though the notion of dying for one's faith retained its currency as a powerful motif throughout Christian history. It can be seen in the crusades and in the idea of a holy quest. Christian soldiers considered themselves willing to die for the cause of bringing their faith to lands now under the sway of Islam, regardless of what we might think of their motivations and theology today. The concept of martyrdom was enough to rally soldiers from far afield in western Europe, men who probably had little concept of the culture they were actually trying to obliterate. Martyrdom became less a consequence of persecution, more an overt demonstration of faith and even a statement of policy – something that remains evident in today's world. The concept of suicide terrorism is a modern reworking of the martyrdom motif, carried out, as it often is, by people with strong religious and political beliefs, eager to make dramatic statements of those beliefs with a view to influencing others.

It is asceticism, however, that has had the most long-lasting effects within the context of the Christian Church today. Celibacy is still read as an indication of holiness in Christian communities, particularly in the Roman Catholic tradition, where it is still a prerequisite for public ministry. Celibate ascetics had come to be regarded as the most holy members of their societies in late antiquity and this concept was transmuted: those who would minister to the society should also be celibate, to prove and perpetuate their own sanctity. The evolution of this notion is evident from the fact that it was not initially Church policy to have a celibate clergy; many very early priests and bishops were married and had their own families. As the Church consolidated its position in the Roman empire, that came to be the exception rather than the rule and eventually church councils began to declare that clergy should be celibate to best devote themselves to God's work. A wife and children were seen as distractions from pastoral duties, sexual desire as a real barrier to true closeness with God. The stance is rigidly maintained by the Catholic branch of Christianity today, as is a certain degree of 'repression' surrounding matters of the body and sexuality. The roots of this lie with those early ascetics who struggled to negotiate a path to salvation in a complex world – a world which many of them did not see lasting much beyond the next generation. While maintaining strict views about their own standards of sanctity, it is unlikely that many individual ascetics intended to dictate church policy in this respect; but admiration for their endeavours in the end elevated their standards of holiness to those for the Christian faithful as a whole.

Another area in which early Christian thinking and the issues behind asceticism influenced more modern church doctrine is in relation to the role of women. This has been well and fully discussed by historians and scholars but it is absolutely clear that a degree of suspicion toward the female sex still remains within Christian circles of authority. Only recently have branches of the Protestant Christian tradition begun to ordain women; dissatisfaction with the move has been so strong among some Protestants that some have transferred to the Catholic tradition, where they can continue to have an all-male priesthood. The origins of this line of thought lay in late antiquity: female ascetics had to work that bit harder just to be favourably compared to men; for Eve's initial 'sin' had contaminated the sex as a whole. So women were unworthy to act as leaders or instructors within the faith: 'for the woman taught the man once, and the fall was the result', said John Chrysostom, using this as the basis for his belief that women should never be allowed to instruct men in doctrinal matters. This feeling of suspicion, reflecting, as it does, contemporary gender-stereotypical roles, has been elevated to the level of divine dogma within Catholicism; and it has only been painfully slow to change in other branches of Christianity.

Ascetics and martyrs were very much a product of their own culture. They responded to the circumstances of the later Roman Empire and indeed were moulded by those circumstances. The Roman world had much stricter notions of appropriate gender roles than modern society; this coloured the thinking of many who wrote and preached extensively during the period. Their teachings have been adopted unchanged by modern church authorities, heedless of the fact that society has now changed substantially. The Roman world of late antiquity was itself in a state of flux. Its inhabitants would have had various anxieties and pressures not in evidence today but nonetheless influencing the thoughts and actions of ascetics and church thinkers then. Perhaps the most interesting aspect of modern Christianity is the way in which actions and thoughts – the products of a particular time, place and specific conditions – have retained the currency of official doctrine long after their original circumstance has changed or even become irrelevant.

Notes

Chapter 1

1. There are even some who think of Socrates as the original martyr, since he was executed for professing certain beliefs. This uses the interpretation of the Greek word *martyr* as one bearing witness to something or to some philosophy; see G. Bowersock, *Martyrdom and Rome* (Cambridge University Press, 1995) ch. 1.
2. For the study of Rome's pantheon and its significance for daily life in the empire, see H. Scullard, *Festivals and Ceremonies of the Roman Republic* (Thames & Hudson, London, 1981); also M. Beard, J. North and S. Price (eds), *Religions in Rome* (Cambridge University Press, 1998) vol. 1.
3. See C. Wells, *The Roman Empire* (Fontana, London, 1984; 2nd edn, 1992) 244.
4. For a detailed study of the various cults and beliefs that became incorporated under the broader heading of Roman paganism, and how this flavoured Roman religion, see R. MacMullen, *Paganism in the Roman Empire* (Yale University Press, 1981).
5. For more on this period in Roman history, and suggestions as to possible causes of the decline of the empire, see D. Kagan, *The End of the Roman Empire* (D.C. Heath & Co., Toronto, 1992); and A.H.M. Jones, *The Decline of the Ancient World* (Longman, Essex, 1966).
6. See R. Markus, *The End of Ancient Christianity* (Cambridge University Press, 1990) ch. 3.

Chapter 2

7. See H. Chadwick, *The Early Church* (Penguin, London, 1967; repr. 1990) ch. 1.
8. For a discussion of Christianity as an 'unacceptable' cult within Roman society, and responses to it as such, see Beard *et al.* (note 2 above) ch. 5.

9. For a more detailed survey of periods of persecution, see R. Lane Fox, *Pagans and Christians* (Penguin, London, 1986) ch. 9.

10. Eusebius, *Church History* 3.33.

11. Eusebius, *Church History* 5.

12. See Lane Fox (note 9 above) 242-3.

13. Eusebius, *Church History* 6.43 and 7.3.

14. E.g. Eusebius, *Church History* 10.7-8.

15. See further J. Salisbury, *Perpetua's Passion* (Routledge, London, 1997) ch. 2.

16. Chadwick (note 7 above) 123-4.

17. Tertullian was writing to Scapula, himself a magistrate guilty of persecuting Christians around AD 212; see also Eusebius, *Church History* 8.9.5. For more on the concept of voluntary martyrdom, see Bowersock (note 1 above) ch. 1; and G.E.M. de Ste Croix, 'Why were the Early Christians Persecuted?' *Past and Present* 26 (1963) 6-38.

Chapter 3

18. P. Veyne, *Bread and Circuses: Historical Sociology and Political Pluralism* (Penguin, London, 1992).

19. For more on martyr texts as a developing form of literature in the Roman empire, see Bowersock (note 1 above).

20. Much has been written on this subject; for particularly good introductions to the issues, see A. Cameron, 'Virginity as Metaphor: Women and the Rhetoric of Early Christianity' in A. Cameron (ed.), *History as Text* (Duckworth, London, 1989) 181-205; C. Pavey, 'The Theology and Leadership of Women in the New Testament'; and R.R. Ruether 'Misogynism and Virginal Feminism in the Fathers of the Church', both in R.R. Ruether (ed.), *Religion and Sexism* (Simon & Schuster, New York, 1974) 117-49 and 150-83 respectively.

21. See J. Perkins, *The Suffering Self: Pain and Narrative Representation in the Early Christian Era* (Routledge, London, 1995).

22. For a more detailed discussion of this issue, see A. Cameron, *Christianity and the Rhetoric of Empire* (University of California Press, 1991).

Chapter 4

23. See also Sozomen, *Ecclesiastical History* 1.4.

24. For laws exempting Christians from municipal duties and financial burdens, and attempts to ensure that only devout and orthodox Christians received the privileges, see *Codex Theodosianus* e.g. 16.2.9 and 16.2.15.

Chapter 5

25. For detailed examination of the role of the physical body in Church thinking, see P. Brown, *The Body and Society: Men, Women and Sexual Renunciation in Early Christianity* (Columbia University Press, 1988).

26. For a review of these theories, see M. Foucault, *History of Sexuality: the Use of Pleasure* (Penguin, London, 1988).

27. See e.g. Augustine, *Sermons* 151.8; or *On The Good of Marriage* 3; and for an examination of Augustine's teaching in this regard, U. Ranke-Heinemann, *Eunuchs for the Kingdom of Heaven* (Penguin, London, 1990) ch. 6.

28. For a study of this phenomenon, see P. Brown, *The Cult of the Saints* (Chicago University Press, 1981); and J. Howard-Johnson and P. Hayward (eds.), *The Cult of Saints in Late Antiquity and the Early Middle Ages: Essays on the Contribution of Peter Brown* (Oxford University Press, 1999), giving a somewhat complex reassessment of Brown's work.

29. Ranke-Heinemann (note 27 above) has particularly strong feelings on this legacy of disgust for human sexuality in the Catholic Church, and on how it has affected the place of women in the organisation.

30. For a review of these arguments and some suggestions of his own, see P. Rousseau, 'Orthodoxy and the Coenobite' *Studia Patristica* 30 (1995) 241-58.

31. Also Evagrius, *Ecclesiastical History* 1.13.

32. For more on Arsenius and other reclusive desert fathers, see B. Ward, *Sayings of the Desert Fathers* (Cistercian Publications, London, 1975).

132

Chapter 6

33. For a review of this phenomenon, see M. Dudley, 'Danger and Glory in the Writing of John Chrysostom' *Studia Patristica* 27 (1991) 162-5.

34. On John's life, see J.N.D. Kelly, *Golden Mouth: the Story of John Chrysostom – Ascetic, Preacher, Bishop* (Duckworth, London, 1995); and for the flavours of ascetic thinking in his preaching, A. Hartney, *Transformation of the City: the Preaching of John Chrysostom* (Duckworth, London, 2004).

35. See D. Greeley, 'John Chrysostom, On the Priesthood: a Model for Service' *Studia Patristica* 22 (1989) 121-8; also T. Urbainczyk, 'Holy Men and Bishops in Theodoret's Religious History' *Studia Patristica* 35 (1999) 167-72.

36. For a complete study of Jerome's career and writings, including his stint in the desert, see J.N.D. Kelly, *Jerome: his Life, Writings and Controversies* (Duckworth, London, 1975).

37. For suggestions as to how to resolve this conflict, see Basil of Caesarea, *Address to Young Men on what Profit may be derived from Pagan Literature*, tr. R. Deferrari (Loeb Classical Library).

38. See P. Cox-Miller, 'The Blazing Body: Ascetic Desire in Jerome's Letter to Eustochium' *Journal of Early Christian Studies* 1.1 (1993) 21-45.

Chapter 7

39. For a review of women's lives in late antiquity, see G. Clark, *Women in Late Antiquity* (Oxford University Press, 1993); and for their legal standing, A. Arjava, *Women and Law in Late Antiquity* (Clarendon Press, Oxford, 1996).

40. See also Jerome, *Against Helvidius: the Perpetual Virginity of the Blessed Mary* 20, (tr. W. Freemantle in *A Select Library of Nicene and post-Nicene Fathers* series 2, vol. 6), which reviews the anxieties and distractions experienced by a typical Roman housewife, which prevent her from focusing properly on God.

41. For a helpful study of female asceticism in the context of other Christian women, see G. Cloke, *This Female Man of God:*

Women and Spiritual Power in the Patristic Age (Routledge, London, 1995).

42. See *Acts of Paul and Thecla*, cited in M. Lewkowitz and M. Fant (eds), *Women's Life in Greece and Rome: a Sourcebook in Translation.* (Duckworth, London, 1995).

43. See *Life of Olympias*, tr. E. Clark in *Jerome, Chrysostom and Friends* (Edwin Mellen Press, New York, 1979).

44. See *Life of Melania the Younger*, tr. E. Clark in *Ascetic Piety and Women's Faith: Studies in Women and Religion* vol. 14 (Edwin Mellen Press, New York, 1984).

45. Similar instructions are contained in Jerome's *Epistle* 107, written to Laeta, a daughter-in-law of Paula, detailing how her own daughter should be raised. She should adhere to the same standards established for Eustochium, if she is to remain in Rome; but Jerome feels it would be still better if she was sent to Bethlehem to live with Paula and Eustochium. There he himself can take personal charge of some parts of her education.

46. For a discussion of the positive effects of asceticism on female lives, see M. Alexandre, 'Early Christian Women' in P. Schmitt Pantel (ed.), *A History of Women* (Belknap Press, Cambridge, Mass.,1992) vol. 1.

47. See Cameron (note 20 above).

48. For more detail on the development of both Eve and Mary as archetypal figures in religious thought, see A. Baring and J. Cashford, *The Myth of the Goddess: Evolution of an Image* (Penguin Arkana, London, 1993) chs 13 and 14. It is interesting to note that popular culture has developed in interest in the way in which the female experience has been written out of the Christian tradition: there is a belief that there exists considerable evidence for the life of Mary, the Mother of God – and for Mary Magdalen's relationship with Jesus; that it has been 'covered up' by subsequent church authorities. Dan Brown's current best-seller, *The Da Vinci Code*, is merely one expression of this school of thought; but the plot of this piece of fiction is firmly rooted in the Gnostic and apocryphal gospels, which we still possess from the early period of church history.

Chapter 8

49. For detailed study of this kind of ascetic, see D. Caner, *Wandering, Begging Monks: Spiritual Authority and the Promotion of Monasticism in Late Antiquity* (University of California Press, 2002).

50. *Life of Alexander the Sleepless*, tr. Caner (note 49 above).

51. See Clark (note 39 above) ch 5.2; and for more detail, S. Brock and S. Harvey, *Holy Women of the Syrian Orient* (University of California Press, 1987).

52. E.g. *The Council of Gangra* canon 13 (mid-fourth century). This is also echoed in secular law: see *Codex Theodosianus* 16.2.27.1.

53. See council rulings against this practice, e.g. *The Council of Nicaea* canon 3: 'this great synod absolutely forbids a bishop, presbyter, deacon or any of the clergy to keep a woman who has been brought in to live with him, with the exception of course of his mother or sister or aunt, or any person who is above suspicion'.

54. For tr. of John Chrysostom's paired treatises on the subject, see Clark (note 43 above); also A. Hartney, 'Manly Women and Womanly Men: the *Subintroductae* and John Chrysostom' in L. James (ed.), *Desire and Denial in Byzantium* (Ashgate Press, London 1999); and for a general review of the topic, Cloke (note 41 above) ch. 4.

Further Reading

Late Antiquity

Peter Brown, *The World of Late Antiquity* (Thames and Hudson, London, 1971; repr. 1999). An excellent and easily accessible guide to the period, and a useful introduction to some of the key issues facing inhabitants of the Roman Empire between AD 150 and 750.

A.H.M. Jones, *The Decline of the Ancient World* (Longman, London, 1966). A more detailed survey of the Rome in late antiquity, with chapters under various headings such as 'Taxation', 'Finance', 'The Church'. It covers a more focused period than Brown's work, and deals specifically with some of the reasons for the decline of the Roman Empire.

Averil Cameron, *The Later Roman Empire* (Fontana Press, London, 1993). A more up-to-date survey of the key topics than Jones' work, and a useful synthesis of scholarship of the period so far, although presented in a very accessible manner.

Donald Kagan, *The End of the Roman Empire; Decline or Transformation* (D.C. Heath & Co., Toronto, 1992). A very useful collection of articles and essays on the period, presenting several approaches to the questions of decline and transformation of the empire during this period.

Peter Garnsey & Averil Cameron (eds), *Cambridge Ancient History XIII* (Cambridge University Press, 1998). An excellent series for providing an overview of key events and issues of the periods in question.

Christianity and the Roman Empire

Henry Chadwick, *The Early Church* (Penguin, London, 1967, repr. 1990). A comprehensive survey of the origins and growth of the Christian Church, and of some of the main religious controversies of the day.

135

Robin Lane Fox, *Pagans and Christians* (Penguin, London, 1986). An excellent and very detailed guide to the growth of Christianity within Roman society, and of the key differences between the Christians and their pagan counterparts. Provides a very good survey of the persecutions and Christian martyrs, but concludes with the conversion of Constantine and its immediate aftermath.

Ramsay MacMullen, *Christianizing the Roman Empire; AD 100-400* (Yale University Press, 1984). An important discussion of the period of transition between the traditional Roman empire and the christianised version. Raises important questions about the extent of conversion to Christianity, and therefore offers a more rounded picture of events.

Averil Cameron, *Christianity and the Rhetoric of Empire; the Development of Christian Discourse* (University of California Press, 1991). A discussion of the complex issue of the christianisation of discourse, and therefore very important for any detailed study of the growth of the Christian religion. The subject matter is intricate, but worth persevering with.

Christian Martyrdom

Herbert Musurillo, *The Acts of the Christian Martyrs; Oxford Early Christian Texts* (Oxford University Press, 1971). A very helpful collection of martyr texts from a variety of periods in Late Antiquity, along with a brief but useful introduction to each text and the key personalities involved.

Joyce Salisbury, *Perpetua's Passion; the Death and Memory of a Young Roman Woman* (Routledge, London, 1997). A portrait of one of the best known early Christian martyrs, as well as a discussion of her social and cultural background. Helpful for the way in which it puts the Christian martyrs in their social context.

Glen Bowersock, *Martyrdom and Rome* (Cambridge University Press, 1995). An accessible discussion of Christian martyrs and their impact on Roman society. Particularly good on the development of martyr texts as a new literary genre.

Christian Asceticism

Peter Brown, *The Cult of the Saints* (University of Chicago Press, 1981). A good introduction to the main precepts of asceticism, and the impact holy men and women had on the landscape of Roman society.

Peter Brown, *The Body and Society; Men, Women and Sexual Renunciation in Early Christianity* (Columbia University Press, New York, 1998). Very detailed discussion of Christian asceticism and its development, and in particular Christian perceptions of the human body, and the influence these perceptions had on subsequent church teachings. A very valuable work.

James Howard-Johnston & Paul A. Hayward (eds.), *The Cult of Saints in Late Antiquity and the Early Middle Ages; Essays on the Contribution of Peter Brown* (Oxford University Press, 1999). A detailed and scholarly work which assesses and updates the work of Peter Brown. Useful for the student who wishes to follow the development of scholarship in this area.

Robert Markus, *The End of Ancient Christianity* (Cambridge University Press, 1990, repr. Canto 1998). Very useful on all areas of the development of Christianity, but has particularly interesting chapters on the impact of asceticism, and its place in the development of medieval Christian thought.

Women and Christianity

Gillian Clark, *Women in Late Antiquity: Pagan and Christian Lifestyles* (Clarendon Press, Oxford, 1993). A detailed survey of women's lives in late antiquity, organised under thematic headings such as law, domesticity, and health.

Gillian Cloke, *This Female Man of God: Women and Spiritual Power in the Patristic Age, AD 350-450* (Routledge, London, 1995). An excellent discussion of the key teachings with regard to women in the early Christian tradition, with reference to many of the chief church writers and leaders of the period.

Uta Ranke-Heinemann, *Eunuchs for the Kingdom of Heaven; Women, Sexuality and the Catholic Church* (Penguin, London, 1990). Although somewhat sensationalist in parts, and very indignant in tone, this book offers an overview of church teachings on women from its origins through to modern history, and is especially helpful on the ways in which the modern Church has been influenced by its past doctrines.

Holy Men and Church Fathers

Vernon Bourke, (ed.), *The Essential Augustine* (Hackett Publishing Company, Indianapolis, 1974). A useful collection of source material drawn from Augustine's writings arranged on a thematic basis, with brief introductions to each idea and its importance to Augustine.

Elizabeth Clark, *Jerome, Chrysostom and Friends* (Edwin Mellen Press, New York, 1979). Useful both for the study of these men themselves, of the roles for women within the early Church, and for translations of several important Church texts on issues surrounding asceticism and the nature of the female sex.

Aideen Hartney, *John Chrysostom and the Transformation of the City* (Duckworth, London 2004). A thematic discussion of the preaching of John Chrysostom, particularly his teachings on social matters such as the roles of the sexes and the uses of wealth in his society.

J.N.D. Kelly, *Jerome: His Life, Writings and Controversies* (Duckworth, London, 1975). A very helpful history of the man, as well as a useful introduction to his writings and their place in the development of Christian doctrine.

J.N.D. Kelly, *Golden Mouth: The Story of John Chrysostom, Ascetic, Preacher, Bishop* (Duckworth, London, 1995). With a similar approach to his work on Jerome, this volume is a very necessary modern guide to an important Church Father.

Anthony Meredith, *The Cappadocians* (St. Vladimir's Seminary Press, New York, 1995). A brief survey of these figures and their main teachings. Useful as a basic introduction.

Philip Rousseau, *Basil of Caesarea* (University of California Press, 1994). A very detailed study of Basil and his writings. Of most use to a student of this particular period in the development of the Eastern Church.

Index

Adam 61, 90
Agape 42
Alexander the Sleepless 113-15
Antony 1, 63-71, 111
apostasy 23, 24-5
Arsenius 76
Asceticism; a denial of physical
        desires and needs as an
        expression of devotion
        57-8, chs. 5 & 6 *passim*
    coenobitic asceticism; a
        community version of
        asceticism 70
    desert asceticism 63-76
    eremitic asceticism; a hermitic
        version of asceticism,
        with protagonists living in
        isolation from society 70
    Syrian asceticism 71-7
    transvestite asceticism 116-18
Athanasius 63-71
Augustine 25, 80, 88-90, 122-3

Basil of Caesarea 89, 95, 96
Blandina 45-7
Blesilla 83
Byzantium 125

Carthage 2, 25, 35
catechumen; a student of the
        Christian faith, awaiting
        baptism 37,
Christianisation of discourse 50
Constantine 15, 31, 32, 51, 52
Constantius 31, 52

Conversion of Constantine 52-4
Cynics, Cynicism 57
Cyprian of Carthage 24, 25

Decius 22, 26, 28, 48
Diocletian 20, 25, 27, 29-31, 43
Donatists 25-6

Epicureanism 5
Essenes 58
Eulalia 43-4
Eusebius, *Ecclesiastical History*
        20, 27, 31-2, 53
Eustochium 102-104
Eve 61, 76, 90, 107, 108-9, 127

Felicity 1, 36-41

Galerius 31-33
Gnostics 58
Gregory of Nyssa 61, 92-8, 107

Hypatia 122-3

Jerome 80, 82-88, 89-90, 95,
        102-104, 106, 111, 116
Jesus 2, 4, 11, 16
John Chrysostom 80-82, 89, 94,
        98-9, 119-20, 127
Judaism 7-8, 36
Julian 63

katharsis 33

Leo 72-3
Libanius 89

Macrina 94-8, 107, 116, 118
Manicheeism 88-90
Marcella 106
Marcus Aurelius 21
Martyrdom 2-4, 12, chs. 2 & 3
       passim, 54-7
   Jewish martyrs 3
   martyrs of Lyon 44-7
   voluntary martyrdom 26-7

Mary 108-110
Maxentius 53
Maximian 31
Maximin 32
Maximinus 22
Melania the Younger 100-101,
     111, 116

Nero 10, 12, 15-17

Olympias 98-100

paganism, traditional Roman
      religion, 4-6, 22, 52
   pagan sacrifice 19-20, 22-3
patrons and clients 54-6
Paul 12, 62
Paula 87, 102-105, 116, 118
Pelagia 117
Perpetua 35-41, 42
persecution chs. 2 &3 passim
Peter 12
Pionius 48-49
Plato 42, 49, 98, 123
Pliny the Younger 17-20
Pythagoras 57

relics 40, 47

Roman citizenship 18-19,
Rule of St. Benedict 75, 113

Sanctus 45-6
Saturus 40
Septimius Severus 8, 9, 36
Simeon Stylites 71-3
Simeon Stylites II 73
Stoicism 5, 57
Stylites 71-5
subintroductae; virgins cohabiting
     with male ascetics in an
     ascetic household 118-20
the fall of Rome 124-7
The Sun god 52, 53
Theodosius I 76
Third century crisis 10, 29-31
Tiberius 7
Trajan 17-20

Valerian 28

wandering monks 75, 112-16

Printed and bound by CPI Group (UK) Ltd, Croydon, CR0 4YY

13/04/2025

14656597-0004